W9-AEX-014

DECORATIVE PAINTING

Painting Realistic Flowers in Acrylic

Arlene Beck

MDA

NORTH LIGHT BOOKS
CINCINNATI, OHIO

About the Author

As a child I can remember eagerly awaiting spring so I could go to the grocery store to buy as many floral seed packets as I could afford. As a teenager I decided to pursue a career in nursing. I made it one of my goals when I graduated from nursing school to paint flowers.

In the seventies, I was encouraged to take classes in tole painting. I had no idea what "tole painting" meant, or what it would mean to me. In this art form I found a wonderful way to learn how to paint without the disappointing failures. I pursued decorative painting classes and painted with many fine artists in the decorative painting field who were willing to share their knowledge and experiences. I became a decorative art teacher, began designing pattern packets, and decided I would gain the credibility I sought if I could achieve a master level in the National Society of Tole and Decorative Painters. I achieved that goal in 1995.

Since then, I have taught decorative art across the United States and Canada and authored a decorative painting pattern book and a full line of pattern packets.

I continue my love affair with flowers. Whenever I feel uncertain about what path I should follow, I always remember that goal I set when graduating from nursing school, and paint flowers.

Painting Realistic Flowers in Acrylic. Copyright © 1998 by Arlene Beck MDA. Manufactured in China. All rights reserved. No part of this book may be reproduced in any form or by any electronic or mechanical means including information storage and retrieval systems without permission in writing from the publisher, except by a reviewer, who may quote brief passages in a review. Published by North Light Books, an imprint of F&W Publications, Inc., 1507 Dana Avenue, Cincinnati, Ohio 45207. (800) 289-0963. First edition.

Other fine North Light Books are available from your local bookstore, art supply store or direct from the publisher.

02 01 00 99 98 5 4 3 2 1

Library of Congress Cataloging-in-Publication Data

Beck, Arlene
    Painting realistic flowers in acrylic / by Arlene Beck.
        p. cm.
    Includes index.
    ISBN 0-89134-776-3 (alk. paper)
    1. Flowers in art. 2. Painting—Technique. I. Title
ND1400.B37 1997
758'.42—dc21   97-17884
                                                               CIP

Edited by Kathy Kipp and Jennifer Long
Production edited by Marilyn Daiker
Designed by Angela Lennert Wilcox

North Light Books are available for sales promotions, premiums and fund-raising use. Special editions or book excerpts can also be created to specification. For details, contact: Special Sales Manager, F&W Publications, 1507 Dana Avenue, Cincinnati, Ohio 45207.

Dedication

This book is dedicated to my mom and dad. Thank you, Mom, for giving me the paint kit; and Dad, thank you for taking the pictures of my first gardens. I would also like to dedicate this book to my husband, Alan, and sons, Kevin and Tim, who have encouraged me and made it easy for me to follow my dreams.

Acknowledgments

I would like to recognize and thank David Lewis for giving me the opportunity to write this book, Greg Albert for his positive attitude and encouragement, Kathy Kipp who listened, understood and kept me going on the right track and all the people at North Light Books whom I never met or talked to, yet who were vital in putting this book together. I would also like to thank Bill Vodek, at Carlyn Studio in Schenectady, New York, for working on the photographs until we had them right.

Table of Contents

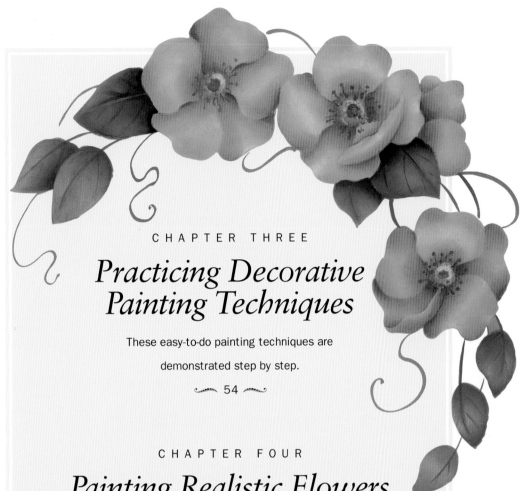

Introduction

One of the most wonderful things about the decorative painting artform is it allows the viewer to appreciate a painting from a distance, or as close as the viewer can get, to enjoy the fine details. This gives the decorative artist the opportunity to paint detail that might otherwise go unnoticed. Those of us who love to paint clean, sharp detail can do just that. This book helps you paint those realistic floral details with acrylics.

To paint flowers that look real, you have to be willing to study them and learn how they grow.

You must learn to see color, be willing to work to execute detail, and be ready to try different approaches and techniques until you find the one that works for you. It may take time to find that technique, but if you're determined, you'll find the discipline to persevere until you do.

I often thought of my discipline as tunnel vision: I said "yes" to the light at the end of the tunnel and "no" to all other exits. Make sure, even if you do exit early a couple of times, you get back in and enjoy the ride.

A Note on Painting Styles

A wonderful aspect of the decorative painting art form is that it encompasses such a large spectrum. For generations, stroke artists all over the world have been painting beautiful items to decorate their homes. From the early American tin decorators to the Norwegian Rosemahlers, many cultures have used painting to personalize and enliven their surroundings.

Even if your goal isn't to become a great stroke artist, the brush control you learn when practicing these strokes is invaluable when climbing to new heights.

When first introduced to the decorative art form, most of us are encouraged by our success and the simple beauty of what we have painted. These initial steps start us on a journey of ever-improving painting skills. In addition, we begin to develop a decorative painting lifestyle and take pride in turning our environment into an expression of ourselves with our art, just as our ancestors did.

Along this creative journey you'll recognize many beautiful, stylized options. When an artist creates an original, unique look, which may or may not be realistic or detailed, it is considered stylized, reflecting that artist's special interpretations.

Remember as you read this book that all styles of decorative painting—from strokework to simple, stylized designs to lifelike, realistically detailed subjects—all have a place in our lives.

However, my goal with this book is to encourage anyone who enjoys decorative art to expand their horizons and see there is always room to grow. There is a natural progression from what seems easy to what appears most difficult, and by the time you get there, it won't seem so difficult after all.

One of the greatest advantages of this art form is you may choose to focus your talent and perfect any area, yet enjoy all. Learning to paint with realistic detail is simply another option for your creativity.

This flower was made with basic stroke work, representing some initial steps in the beautiful and complex stroke designs. It contains flat brush petals, line work, stroke leaves and small comma strokes.

This blossom can be painted by beginner painters and used to decorate any small functional piece or as a repeating border. Line work separates the crescent stroke petals and indicates veins in the small stroke leaves. The center is stippled.

This flower represents a stylized, yet more realistic look. Petals are basecoated, shaded around the center and highlighted along the outside. The center is stippled using two values to give it more dimension. The center is further detailed using dots as stamens and pistils. The leaves use dark and light values to create depth and indicate form.

This blossom, although still stylized, has an even more realistic look. The petals and leaves roll and lift because of proper value placement. Fine line work creates detail, and the stamens and pistils have been given a more precise, realistic rendering. The center has three values, there are tints and accents on the petals and leaves, and temperature change has been used to position the leaves and draw attention to the desired petals.

CHAPTER ONE

Getting Started

Brushes

One of the most common questions my students ask is "what brushes should I use?" It reminds me of the days when I was buying brushes with my grocery money and was forced to learn how to use and control the brushes I had on hand. Many of you probably have a large assortment of brushes you just had to have to paint that beautiful picture, but because you never learned how to control those brushes, they're stored in your brush case, brought out occasionally to be admired and put back. You then proceed to paint with the *old favorite*. If that old favorite is the brush you have learned to control, the one you are most successful with, then use it! The bottom line is control and success.

However, if you aren't experiencing success with your brushes, paints and mediums, be willing to try new materials and develop new skills. I just want you to remember success isn't always easy.

I use an assortment of Loew-Cornell Golden Taklon flat, round and liner brushes. They hold a good amount of water and last a long time with proper care and cleaning. I use the 7350 series liner, no. 1 and no. 2; the 7000 series round, no. 3 and no. 5; and the 7300 series shader no. 2 through no. 12. I also keep old, scruffy flat brushes handy for various tasks. I have several soft, round sable brushes I use to help soften and blend values—I usually use Langnickel's Royal Sable 5005 series round no. 6, no. 10 and no. 14.

Paint

I use Delta Ceramcoat Acrylic Paints almost exclusively. These water-based paints are sold in bottles and are nontoxic.

It is necessary to shake the bottles of paint before use as the medium and resins tend to rise to the top. Keep your paint out of direct sunlight and freezing temperatures, and avoid storing them next to heating vents or in the car.

I use FolkArt Extender. I find this the easiest of the extenders to use, although I use different retarding products when I want a longer drying time.

For my techniques, a disposable waxed palette works best. I avoid stay-wet palettes because the extra water involved tends to dilute the retarding properties of the extender.

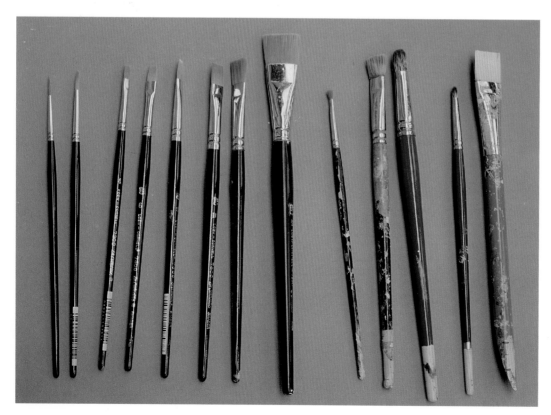

Brushes I use an assortment of flat and round brushes. I have several scruffy brushes I use for different tasks and short sable rounds I use to soften edges.

Brush Basin

I like to use a three compartment brush basin for several reasons: It keeps my brush immersed in water below the ferrule to prevent paint from drying in my brush, provides an area for clean water and an area to rinse the brush in. Using the brush basin has increased the longevity of my brushes because acrylic paint dries quickly in brush hairs if they are not cleaned properly or kept wet. To clean my brushes, I apply Houston Art & Frame Pink Soap to my palette and stroke the brush into the soap as if I were loading the brush with paint. I never smash the brush straight down into the soap or clean the brushes in my hand. On the occasions that I have accidently let paint dry in my brush, I tried to salvage the brush by cleaning it with rubbing alcohol in the same manner as described above.

Attitude

I think attitude has a lot to do with success. You must realize that it takes time to polish and develop skills, understand theory and do the boring preparations, and that there will be times even when you're an experienced painter when you'll be unhappy with what you've painted. But if you are determined and keep at it, you will succeed.

Surfaces, Preparations and Finishes

I most frequently paint on wooden surfaces. I find the base coat paint tends to soften and lift with many of the techniques I use when applying it to Masonite and tin. I use a canvas when a smooth surface and thin layers of paint aren't necessary.

When I prepare a surface, sand between basecoats or apply a finish, I use 600-grit sandpaper. I then use a tack cloth to remove sanding dust and lint.

When sealing wooden surfaces, I use Designs from the Heart wood sealer because it penetrates the surface of the wood. To finish a painting, I generally use Delta Ceramcoat Satin Varnish.

Tracing and Transferring Supplies

As tempting as it can be to use a pattern as is, I find it much more accurate to trace the pattern onto tracing paper first. There are several kinds of graphite paper on the market—I prefer gray graphite. When starting with a new piece, I always wipe away some of the excess graphite with a paper towel. Graphite paper can be used over and over, as lighter lines are preferable. I use the fine tip of a stylus to transfer patterns to the surface.

Since pencil eraser can mar or abrade a surface and a rubber eraser can leave lots of pills, I use a soft white eraser to take off pattern lines.

Miscellaneous Supplies

Other miscellaneous supplies include a small cup for extender, paper towels, Krylon #1311 Matte Finish spray coating, a magnifying glass, wood putty and sponge brushes.

I use warm and cool light (both incandescent and florescent).

Setting Up

I always set up my painting area the same way—it's convenient and makes painting easier. I'm right-handed, so I keep my setup on my right side in a convenient location. I arrange my supplies so I can go from basin to paper towel to palette in a smooth action. Avoid setting your palette where you will have to cross your body and/or project to reach it. Keep your paper towel—an important tool—close to your basin, not in your hand.

Preparing Wood and Other Surfaces

When preparing a wooden surface, begin by filling any nail holes or marks with wood putty following the manufacturer's instructions. When the putty is dry, sand the surface smooth and wipe it with a tack rag. "Tack" the surface after every sanding. Seal all wood surfaces with wood sealer using a sponge brush. When dry, sand lightly and tack again.

I also lightly sand canvas surfaces to remove any loose knobs before painting. If painting on a Masonite panel, tack the surface, then spray it lightly with Krylon #1311 Matte Finish before basecoating.

I recommend choosing preprimed tin over a raw tin surface—you will save hours of preparation. As with Masonite, I recommend lightly misting a tin surface with Krylon #1311 Matte Finish before basecoating.

Basecoating

Use as large a brush as possible to basecoat a background surface. This keeps the surface smooth. If a ridge or overlap forms, quickly swipe over it into the wet paint. Basecoating with a damp brush also helps to avoid brush marks. If you feel the paint is dragging or is too stiff, pick up more water in your brush.

When basecoating individual objects in a design, use the largest brush you can as this helps prevent overlaps. I treat a flower as one unit when basecoating—basecoating petal by petal may cause ridges. Avoid using small liner or round brushes on large areas because this will cause ridges and overlaps. You want the surface to be as smooth as possible, making sure there are no ridges along outside edges of objects. I always basecoat at least twice to achieve an opaque coverage, sanding and tacking between coats. When basecoating on a dark background, you may need more that two coats.

Even though the paint is dry to the touch in about half an hour, it takes up to twenty-four hours for the paint to

Basic set up
Keep your supplies convenient and easy to reach.

Basecoating
If ridges do occur when basecoating, swipe into the wet paint with your finger.

Use a damp brush and shorter strokes when basecoating. You will get a smoother surface using paint thinned with a little water. It will be much easier to apply two thin basecoats than to try to sand smooth a thick, rough surface or to paint over an uneven surface.

Avoid using a round or liner brush to basecoat; they can cause overlaps and ridges. When touching up a small area, it's tempting to use a small liner, but you will be better off using a corner load in a small flat brush.

properly cure and achieve a hard surface. I want a hard surface because it helps prevent the graphite pattern lines from becoming imbedded in the paint, but like many of you I usually don't have twenty-four hours to wait for the paint to cure, so instead I lightly spray the surface with Krylon #1311 Matte Finish. This coat also helps prevent graphite smudges from embedding into the surface from what I call palming it during the transfer process.

Transferring a Pattern

I feel it's important to trace a pattern onto transfer paper instead of working directly from the original pattern. It enables you to see the surface so you can align the design correctly, helps keep your touch lighter when transferring the pattern, saves the original pattern for future use, and gives you the opportunity to proof the design and make corrections.

The most important thing when tracing a pattern is to be accurate. I try to make sure edges are rounded, or straight and angular, when they're supposed to be. While tracing the pattern, I have a chance to study the design before painting. Tracing with a sharp pencil gives me the opportunity to erase and make changes in the tracing, and also saves on distortion caused by a wider, thicker pen or pencil. Once traced, I proof the pattern and ask myself if it will be pleasing if I paint it exactly as I see it.

Before transferring a pattern, tape the tracing to the surface. You can then lift the tracing without worrying about the pattern shifting and realigning incorrectly. Slip the graphite paper between the surface and the tracing, and transfer the pattern using a stylus with as light a touch as possible. Erase any dark graphite lines.

Taping your tracing to your surface will prevent your design from shifting when inserting graphite paper and tracing. Even a shift of a fraction of an inch can cause a large distortion on a small pattern area.

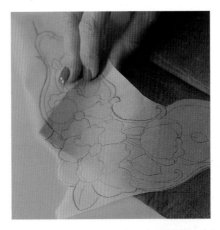

Carefully insert graphite paper between your tracing and the surface.

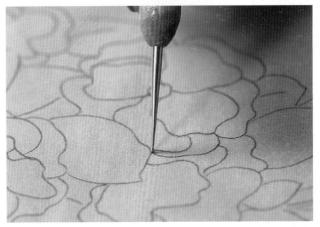

Using a fine-point tool and a light touch, transfer the design to your surface. Remember to keep your graphite lines as light as possible so they won't be visible in the finished painting.

Getting in the Right Mood

I make sure I'm comfortable before I begin to paint. If I find I'm not painting like I want to and warm-up exercises don't help, I leave my project and come back later. I often use this time to seal, basecoat or finish other pieces.

CHAPTER TWO

Understanding the Basics of Realistic Painting

For years, every time I saw a flower I would imagine painting the delicate ruffle, the interesting center and the fine vein lines just the way I saw them. I wanted to capture as much of that detail as I could.

In order to paint a truly realistic painting, you must not only be familiar with your subject, but you must also understand some basic principles of design. I know this may sound intimidating, but you will soon find that these concepts are much less complicated than you imagined, and that painting is much easier once you know what you're trying to accomplish and why.

Knowing Your Subject Matter

Before I start to paint any flower, let alone a flower with realistic details, I make sure I know my subject matter. It's important to understand that in order to paint an object, whether it is a dog, flower or lamp, it is necessary to know your subject.

I have lots and lots of photographs I have taken of flowers and other subjects, as well as interesting lighting and shadows, that I use for reference. I like to take my own photographs, then during the long winter months when there are no flowers in bloom, I have my own reference source. I use a Pentex P30t with a 28-78mm zoom lens, 100 speed film and a tripod.

I also have many reference and gardening books and seed catalogs I use as resources, but I avoid painting directly from any of them. Since nothing compares to a live model, whenever I have the opportunity I visit gardens to study flowers—from their leaves, centers and colors to the way they grow and sway with a breeze. On these visits I often take notes describing how the light flows through a petal or a shadow is cast. Many varieties of flowers are also available from florists.

I took this shot to remind myself how these petals ruffle and roll.

In this shot I captured the small cast shadows where the petals appear to cut into the flower. The large cast shadow is also interesting—notice the transparency and the cool blue color.

Photographs like these are good references when you're working on intricate details like the stamen and pistil.

Many petals form a cup as they open. The rose petal forms a cup, but the edge rolls out and over. Note as many details as you can about each flower as you photograph or study it, such as the thin light line on the smaller rose which is actually the thickness of the petal.

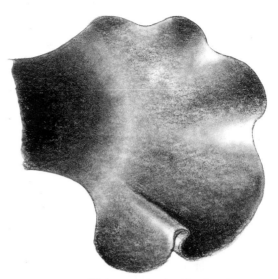

Because of their structure and detail, most flowers are intimidating to paint at first. I find if I study a flower carefully enough, the thought of painting it is not so intimidating. I've always had a zinnia bed, but I have shied away from painting the zinnias because there are so many petals I felt it would be an overwhelming task. When I finally did include them in a painting, I was amazed at how easy they were to paint. It's like having a "one day at a time" attitude.

Sometimes I sketch an enlarged petal or center to help me see where I'm going before I start. I may also do a value sketch to help me get a better feel for my subject.

If it becomes hard to identify value changes because the flower, petals or details are too small, try enlarging them so they become clearer. Study how the petals roll and the values change.

By enlarging this flower it becomes easier to see how the petals relate to each other and where the darkest and lightest values fall.

Recognizing Characteristic Details

In order to paint realistic flowers, it's important to recognize a flower's identifying characteristics. There are many flowers you can easily recognize just by the shape of the petals or the way they grow. Are they vines? Do they creep low to the ground? Do they grow straight on tall stalks like an iris? Do they have rather short stems like pansies? If it is a tall, spiky flower, do the florets grow up like lupines or down like foxglove, or maybe all around the stalk like delphinium? Petals can roll, curl or be stiff. Some flowers have very large petals, like an iris or tiger lily. Some flowers have single petals, like a fruit blossom, while others have several rows of petals, like a zinnia. Queen Anne's lace and yarrow have several clusters of small flowers that make up larger clusters, which in turn make up one even larger cluster. Roses have several petals that connect to form a globular blossom.

Half of the battle is won when these identifying characteristics are pinpointed. For example, when I talk about a flower with rolling petals, thorns and saw-tooth edged leaves, I have described a rose. A cone-shaped flower that grows on a vine and has a rolled edge and light streaks in the petals is a morning glory. An Easter lily can be recognized as a large white blossom having dark yellow stamen and pistils, several blossoms on a stalk and narrow, smooth, long leaves. If these details are painted with attention, the viewer will have no problem recognizing and enjoying the subject matter.

The blossoms on the foxglove grow all around and down the stalk.

Delphinium blossoms also grow around the stalk.

The zinnia has several rows of tight petals. Be sure to notice the center and how the petals seem to cup and roll out. The leaves and cast shadows are also worth studying.

Queen Anne's lace grows in small clusters that form one unit.

The lily has large petals and an interesting center with apparent cast shadows. Notice the values on the petals as they roll and tip down.

Placing the Details

When I think of details I think of color, leaves, tendrils, centers, water drops, veining, bug "bites," buds and any other feature that identifies a specific flower. Although it would be interesting to paint every flower in a design with equal amounts of detail, it could be potentially dangerous. One of the purposes of detail in a painting is to help draw and keep a viewer's attention in an area. I use detail to draw the viewer's eye to the center of interest.

The center of interest is not necessarily one object, but an area in a painting. When determining the center of interest I use *The Rule of Thirds*. After the center of inter-

est area has been established, everything else is positioned in relationship to that area. The center of interest area will have the most detail; areas moving away from the center will have less and less detail.

Once viewers have explored the center of interest, detail can help carry their eye through the painting and then back to the center of interest. If there is too much detail outside the center of interest area, it can be distracting and actually cause the viewer's eye to leave the painting. I'm not saying leave out all detail in the peripheral areas; just use less in relation to that established in the center of interest.

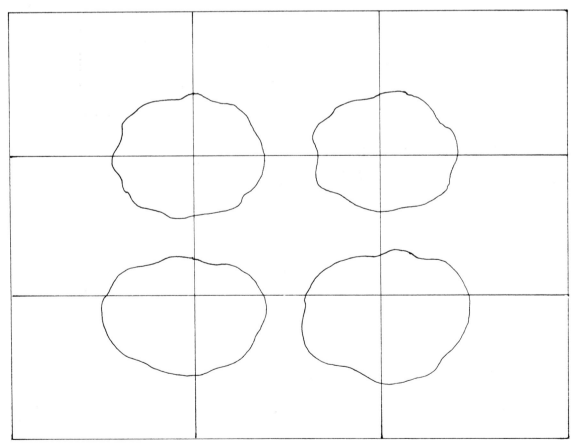

The Rule of Thirds Divide your surface into three equal parts both vertically and horizontally. The four points where these lines intersect make good areas for your center of interest. This rule prevents you from placing the center of interest in the exact center of your surface and helps to keep the design equidistant from the edges.

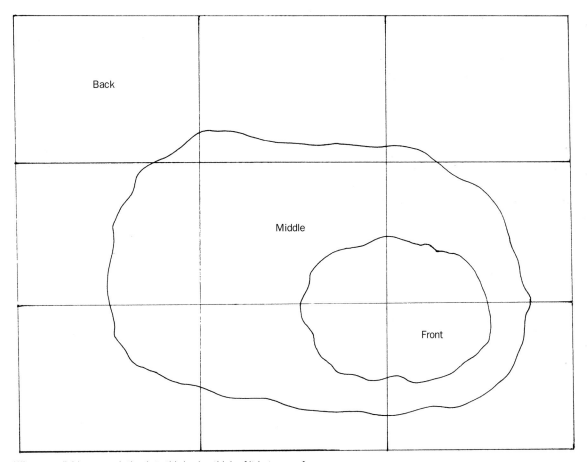

When you divide your painting into thirds also think of it in terms of dividing the painting into three-dimensional planes. The front plane (the one closest to you) is where the center of interest and the most detail is located, the middle plane has less detail, and finally the back or farthest plane has only minimal detail.

Value

Detail isn't the only element that spotlights your painting's center of interest. Color is also a very important element in your overall design. It is therefore necessary to understand some basic concepts about color, including value, intensity and temperature.

Value is the lightness or darkness of an object. Many artists refer to this lightness and darkness as tone. Value is the most important aspect in a painting because value change creates the appearance of three dimensional objects on two dimensional surfaces. Value change is necessary to create a center of interest. The darkest darks and lightest lights fall in the center of interest area.

The overall value of a painting can affect how we feel about the painting: a dark dramatic painting can make us feel melancholy or serious while a light painting can make us feel happy or serene.

Gray Scale

Value changes, or changes in lightness and darkness, can be compared on a chart detailing shades of gray. This chart is called a value scale. The value scale includes black (numbered zero), white (numbered ten) and nine equidistant shades of gray. All colors can be compared to this scale and their value identified. Not all colors are a perfect number two or three, they may fall anywhere in between.

In a low-key painting—one painted mostly in dark values—the lightest value may be a value number seven, while in a high-key painting, one painted in light values, the darkest value may be between values number three and four.

The easiest way to determine the value of a color is to paint your own value scale. Using a flexible surface like bristol board or heavy watercolor paper, measure a strip 2" (5cm) wide by 11" (27.9cm) long and divide the length into eleven one-inch parts. Start by painting the bottom pure black and the top pure white. Begin mixing black and white to create the different values of gray. I would like to tell you that you use equal parts of black and white to reach the middle value, but I find I have to use more white than black. As you are mixing these grays, strive for what appears to be equal gradations in lightness or darkness between values. When you look at the completed scale, you should see an even, gradual change from dark to light.

Once the paint is dry, punch a hole into the center of each value. Now place the holes one by one over the color in question and ask yourself if the color showing through is lighter or darker than the surrounding value. When you can say the color is neither lighter nor darker than the square on the scale, you have found its value.

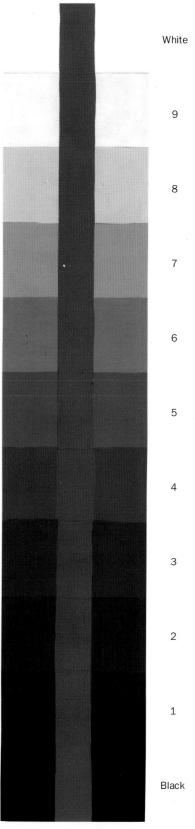

White

9

8

7

6

5

4

3

2

1

Black

Compare a color to a gray scale to determine its value. Use this tool as a guide when evaluating value change. Let it help you train your eye to make good value transitions.

The value of colors in a low-key painting may range between one and seven.

The darkest value in a high-key painting may be a three or four. This type of color scheme is often referred to as pastel because of its light values.

Another Trick for Seeing Values
By squinting at an object until your vision becomes hazy or blurs, you can eliminate some of the color, thereby seeing the value more clearly.

Value Change to Create Form

Look at a round object. The side furthest from the light source is receiving the least light, and therefore is darkest, while the area most directly in the light is lightest in color. In between are gradations from the darkest dark to the lightest light. It is this gradual change from darkest to lightest value that creates form in our paintings. All the dark values fall in the dark value area and the light values fall in the light value area. If they overlap, you'll get a dull muddy look.

I almost always use an upper right center light source. When light hits an object straight on, it tends to flatten the object. Be consistent no matter what direction your light is coming from.

An object must have a minimum of three value changes to have dimension: a light value, a middle value and a dark value. The most value changes should occur in the center of interest area. Since this is also where the most detail is located, some objects in this area may have more than ten value changes.

Generally I basecoat objects in a low, light value. The

middle value is the value we perceive the object to be. I can then shade, and add shadows and folds with my darker values. I find it easier to shade with acrylic paint than to apply highlights, as highlights tend to become milky or chalky.

The first value shading, no matter how it is applied, must connect the basecoat value and the shading values. This application must be transparent enough to bridge the transition line between the shaded area and the basecoat color. If the basecoat value is a value six and the first value shading is a value four, you have to establish the missing value five by painting a thin layer of value five paint on that area. Each application of darker shading value paint covers a smaller and smaller area. The same applies to highlights—each application of light value paint covers a smaller and smaller area. If you do not carry the initial layers of paint out far enough on an object, and just keep applying one shading or highlighting value on top of the next, you end up with a very dark or very light stripe or bullseye.

Gradual value change causes this circle or sphere—as well as the other three basic shapes that follow—to have dimension.

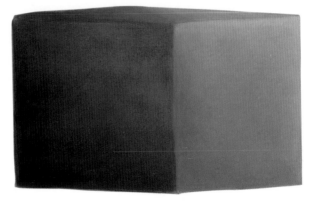

A cube or box.

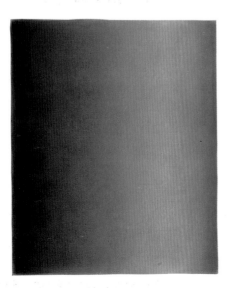

A cylinder.

A cone or triangle.

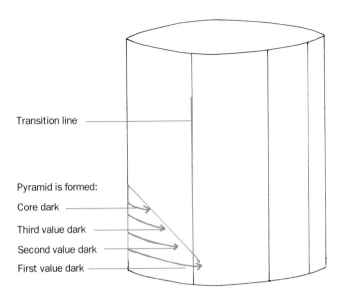

Transition line

Pyramid is formed:

Core dark

Third value dark

Second value dark

First value dark

The first value dark must extend or cover the biggest area. The next application of paint will not extend as far out on the surface. The following application of paint will cover even less area, and the final darkest dark, sometimes referred to as the core dark, covers even less space. Notice how a "pyramid" is formed as the values cover less and less area. This is how you pyramid your colors.

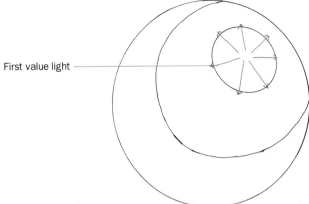

First value light

The first application of light value covers the largest area. Be sure to pull paint out onto the object.

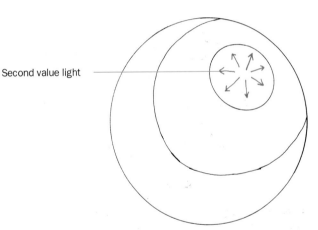

Second value light

The next application covers less area.

Light Source

In nature, there is only one light source—the sun. All light travels in a straight line; it can not bend around corners or curves. The placement of light and dark values is directly related to the direction of the light source. As light passes over an object, the area closest to the light source will be the lightest. Once the object starts to turn it is no longer illuminated by direct light and becomes the shadow area. Light that bounces back off surrounding objects illuminating the shadow side is called reflected light.

Final light value highlight

The final value light or highlight will cover the least area and complete the "pyramid."

Shadows

Shadows create interest in a painting, and help define and anchor an object. I mention them here because even shadows have value changes.

There are two types of shadows: body shadows and cast shadows. The dark side of an object, the side away from the light source is the body shadow. Cast shadows are caused when direct light is interrupted by an object, the object creating a shadow on the area where the light is blocked.

The darkest area of a shadow is where the object and the shadow meet, and the shadow tends to become lighter as it moves away from the object. If an object is lying on a table, it is necessary to paint a solid dark line where it meets the surface. Otherwise the object will appear to float.

Shadows appear lighter when the light is soft and far away, and become darker the closer the light is to the object. Many times a shadow seems lighter toward the center area or where reflected light is illuminating the surface more.

We tend to think of shadows as being colorless, cool and dark, but in reality shadows can be warm, light and contain many colors. Because shadows fall on lighted surfaces, which are warm, by comparison we get the impression that shadows are cool, when actually the outside edge may appear cool and the interior warmer.

Cast shadows will always be darker than the surface they are cast upon. The color of a cast shadow is not determined by the object that is casting the shadow, but by the color of the surface it is shading—only duller and darker. It therefore makes sense to paint the shadow with the complement of the surface color and darken it with a darker gray mix. If you study cast shadows it's obvious the shadow is transparent—you can still identify details on the surface. To create the illusion of a shadow, you must keep it transparent.

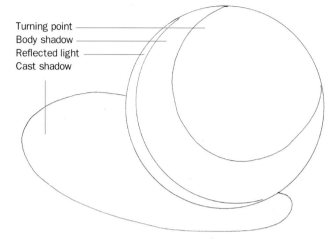

Turning point
Body shadow
Reflected light
Cast shadow

The body shadow is found where the object is no longer illuminated by direct light. The cast shadow is darkest where it meets the object and then continues to have gradual value change. The turning point is where the object starts to turn away from direct light.

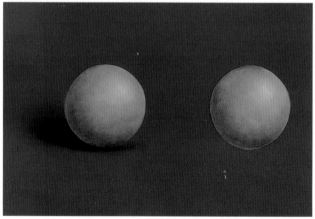

You must paint a dark line where an object meets a surface, then gradually change the value as it moves away from the object or it will appear to float, as the ball on the right does.

Basic Shapes

You may be thinking that establishing values on basic shapes, as I have done on page 26, looks easy enough, but what about complicated objects like flowers and leaves? The key is to break complicated subjects into basic shapes before you try to establish their values.

There are four basic shapes that all objects can be broken down into: a square or cube, a circle or sphere, a triangle or cone and a rectangle or cylinder. When I first heard everything could be broken down into one of these four shapes, I found it confusing. But with a little imagination, I began to see cylinders in ribbons and leaves, and cones in school bell handles. Be willing to really *see* what you're looking at.

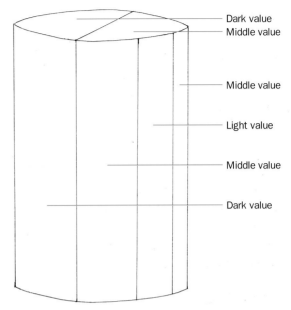

Value placement on a cylinder. The cylinder may be placed in a horizontal or diagonal direction, but value placement remains consistent.

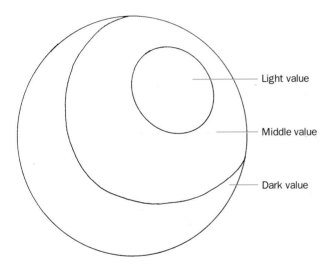

Value placement on a circle. The value placement remains the same as long as the light source remains constant.

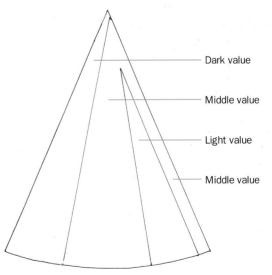

Value placement on a cone.

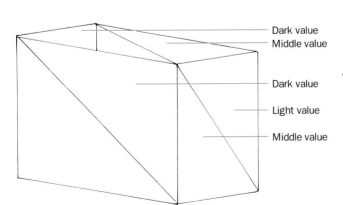

Value placement on a box.

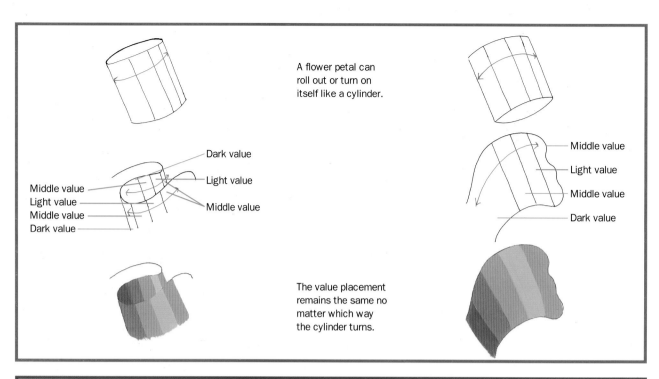

A flower petal can roll out or turn on itself like a cylinder.

Dark value
Light value
Middle value

Middle value
Light value
Middle value
Dark value

Middle value
Light value
Middle value
Dark value

The value placement remains the same no matter which way the cylinder turns.

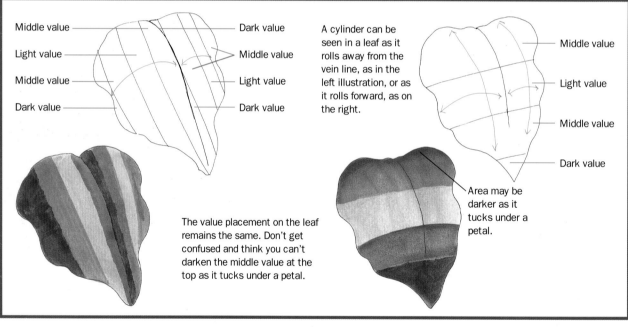

Middle value
Light value
Middle value
Dark value

Dark value
Middle value
Light value
Dark value

A cylinder can be seen in a leaf as it rolls away from the vein line, as in the left illustration, or as it rolls forward, as on the right.

Middle value
Light value
Middle value
Dark value

Area may be darker as it tucks under a petal.

The value placement on the leaf remains the same. Don't get confused and think you can't darken the middle value at the top as it tucks under a petal.

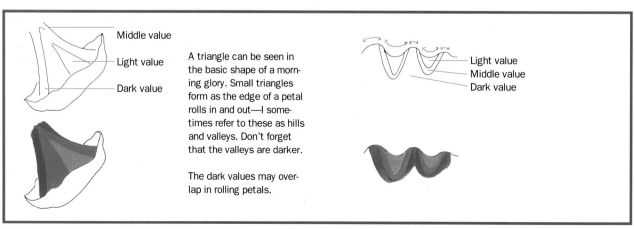

Middle value
Light value
Dark value

A triangle can be seen in the basic shape of a morning glory. Small triangles form as the edge of a petal rolls in and out—I sometimes refer to these as hills and valleys. Don't forget that the valleys are darker.

The dark values may overlap in rolling petals.

Light value
Middle value
Dark value

When painting florals, it is critical to remember that often there are several shapes within one blossom. For example, a rose blossom is basically a sphere and the petals are cylinders or smaller spheres. Paint each individual sphere with at least three value changes. All the petals in the light value area of the large sphere have at least three value changes within that light value range, all the petals in the middle value area of the large sphere have at least three value changes within the middle value range and all the petals in the dark value area of the large sphere have at least three value changes within that dark value range.

It is necessary to understand the importance of painting the basic shapes of the flower and petals with good value control— you have to create a flower before you can ruffle its petals.

When you start to paint a rose or globular flower, think of the whole flower as a single object with value changes before you start painting the individual petals. The values of the petals have to correspond to their placement within the value range of the whole flower.

Light value area

Antique White

Flesh Tone

Island Coral

Middle value area

Flesh Tone

Island Coral

Desert Sun

Dark value area

Island Coral

Desert Sun

Cayeene

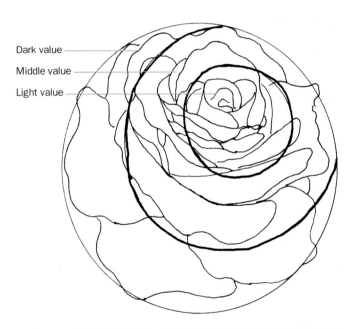

Dark value

Middle value

Light value

For example, the three basic values of the petals in the light value area of the rose may be Antique White, Flesh Tone and Island Coral. Flesh Tone, Island Coral and Desert Sun might be used in the middle value area. Island Coral, Desert Sun and Cayeene might make up the petal values in the dark value area. Just because you change values doesn't mean you can't repeat a value in a darker or lighter area.

Background Value

When considering the values of the objects in your painting, remember that these choices must relate to the background value in order to create a sense of depth. On a dark background light values come forward and dark values recede, and on a light background dark values come forward and light colors recede. If you painted a mid-value stripe along the length of your gray scale, you would see that in the dark value area, it appears lighter and in the light value area, it appears darker.

On a light background light objects will recede and dark objects will come forward.

On a dark background dark objects will recede and light objects will come forward.

Relating Objects' Values to Each Other

Another factor to consider when deciding the values of an object is that objects in the same plane are generally of equal value. To keep an object in the background, keep its value close to the background's value. As objects move toward the foreground, there will be more value changes. The most value changes occur in the front or closest plane, where you should find the lightest lights and darkest darks.

When determining the value of an object, be sure to consider its placement in the painting in relation to other objects. There should be a gradual change in value as you leave the center of interest, so the viewer's eye can travel through a painting, not just bounce around from one area of great contrast to another.

You can separate objects on the same plane with detail, temperature or intensity. This is important to remember when you want to separate several petals on one flower. Let's talk about intensity now.

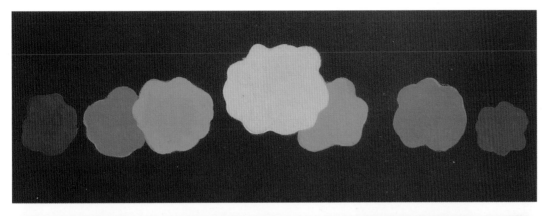

The values of all objects in a painting should be in relation to the center of interest. There should be a gradual change in values so the viewer's eye can travel through the painting.

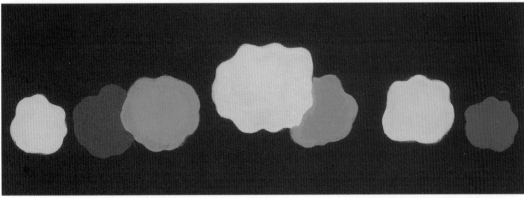

If there is not a good value change the viewer's eye will bounce back and forth from one area of great contrast to another.

Avoid making one object so light or dark that it creates too much contrast, causing your viewer's eye to stop, rather than travel to surrounding areas.

Intensity

Intensity is the second element of color theory. Intensity is the brightness or dullness of a color. When determining the intensity of a color, don't confuse light with bright or dark with dull. A color can be very dark and still be very bright. The most intense colors should be found in the center of interest area, along with all that detail, because they demand the viewer's eye, but may not keep it there very long if it is too intense and not handled well. On the other hand, a dull flower looks like it is dying or dried.

The only way a color can be made more intense is to add more pure pigment from that color family. Generally, the purer the pigment in bottled acrylics, the more trans-parent the paint. You should use this fact to your advantage. Have you ever tried to lighten an object only to have it become too chalky or too milky? Or have you ever painted a flower that appeared too dull or lifeless? One of the best solutions to bump the intensity back up is to paint a light wash of transparent paint from the same family over it.

Bottled colors are often toned or grayed to create a variety of subtle shades, and may contain resins or additives that affect the pigment. Yet they are still very dull or intense, and not exactly what you need in a painting. You may need to rely on complementary colors to create intensity in your painting if you are using bottled acrylics.

A color can be light and still be dull or bright, just as a dark color can be dull and bright. Dark does not mean dull. Many dark colors can be very bright and remain bright when diluted to shade. However, some dark colors are very dull and need to be diluted with water or mixed with white to determine their intensity.

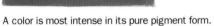

A color is most intense in its pure pigment form.

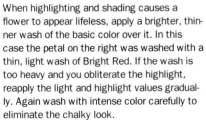

When highlighting and shading causes a flower to appear lifeless, apply a brighter, thinner wash of the basic color over it. In this case the petal on the right was washed with a thin, light wash of Bright Red. If the wash is too heavy and you obliterate the highlight, reapply the light and highlight values gradually. Again wash with intense color carefully to eliminate the chalky look.

Complementary Colors

A color can be made to appear more intense by setting it next to its complement. A color's complement falls opposite it on the color wheel. When you place complementary colors next to each other, they set off a vibration that makes them appear more intense and affects how we feel and relate to those combinations. We see and use this concept daily. Christmas decorations are red and green; in the spring, everything comes up in yellows and purples; and you can't walk down an aisle in the supermarket without spotting a bright orange and blue detergent or cereal box.

The next time you pick up a magazine or watch a television commercial, notice how intense the colors are and how they are used to excite our imagination and desire. Employ this strategy when deciding what colors you will use in the center of interest.

In addition, painting a touch of a color's complement in the light value area will cause a vibration and make it appear brighter; however, don't paint a bold green highlight on a red flower—you don't want the complementary color to be obvious.

A color can appear more intense when placed next to its complement. Use a color's complement to shade near the center of interest, or to dull the colors in the center of a flower.

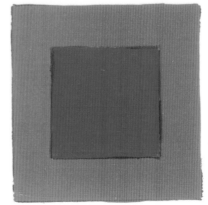

Controlling Intensity

Just like value, it's important to control intensity in your painting so the viewer's eye will flow throughout the painting. You really don't want bright red flags popping up in your painting. Often we see a bottled color that appears pleasing and we can't wait to basecoat the background of our next project with it, but we're disappointed to find that in a large area the color is so intense it's shouting at you! As a color covers more area and dries, it can appear more intense. If you understand how to control intensity you can adjust that color so that it suits your purpose.

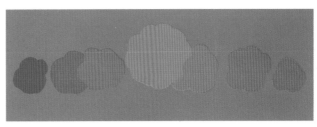

When intensity is controlled it can draw the viewer's eye to the center of interest and lead them gradually throughout the painting.

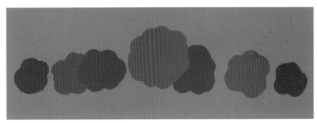

The intensity of various objects in a painting can cause a viewer's eye to jump from one area to another.

Too many or too intense objects can divide a painting or cause the viewer's eye to stop and then leave the painting.

As a background color dries it can appear darker and more intense. A background that is too intense can be distracting and not relate well to your painting.

There are lots of options available when trying to control intensity. When I want to dull a color, I first try adding some of the background color to it. This not only dulls, it also sets objects into the background. This may not work if you want the object to remain on the same picture plane. Because a blossom is the background for the flower center, and leaves are the background for a flower, I treat them as a background color.

Gray can also dull a color. This works well when you add it to the complementary color to dull a color for a body or cast shadow. It also can add a neutral color to a group of leaves. Because you can control the value of the gray mix, it works with the established value.

Adding black to darken the color can also control intensity. But be careful, some colors change color families when mixed with black.

Most basecoat or middle values have some white added to them. White not only lightens, but also dulls a color.

However, if you are happy with the value of your object you shouldn't use white because it raises the value.

One of the most obvious ways of neutralizing a color is to add its complement. Adding two complementary colors in the correct proportions creates a neutral gray.

Also try adding a color's neighbor on the color wheel to dull the intensity of an object. The intensity of the object as a whole may not be affected as that color is added, but the original color won't be as intense. You can also try adding the neighboring leaf or flower color to the color you want to dull.

Earth colors are wonderful colors to use to decrease intensity. They're called earth colors because they are made with chemicals from the earth. Just by their nature, they are duller and generally weaker colors. In bottled acrylics, the colors we assume to be earth colors may have additives that alter them, so experiment to see which ones work in your situation.

One of your best options to control intensity is to add the background color to your mixture, especially in the peripheral areas or in the middle plane when two objects hold the same value.

When you want to save the value of a flower or leaf but change the intensity, try adding a gray of equal value to the mixture.

Black will decrease the intensity of a color, but it may also change the color family.

 Yellow and Black

 Bright Red and Black

 Hydrangea Pink and Black

Notice how yellow and black make green, and when black is added to red the resulting color is purple. The value of a color does not change this. Pink turns lavender when black is added.

If you want to raise the value of a color and decrease the intensity, add white.

Neutral Colors

When complementary colors are mixed they will neutralize each other. When you can no longer recognize either color you have reached a neutral color. This may be hard to identify until you add white. Notice how these neutral colors make some of the nicest beiges or basecoat tans.

Yellow	Orange	Bright Red	Purple	Ultra Blue	Kelly Green

When you add a neighboring color from the color wheel, you automatically get a cool and warm variation of the color. When applying this to a painting, I also consider a neighboring color to be the color of the flower, leaf or object next to the object I am painting.

$\mathcal{F}$inally, because of the nature of acrylic paint, you can decrease the intensity by simply adding more water to your brush and thereby decreasing the amount of pigment.

| Yellow and Pigskin | Orange and Burnt Sienna | Bright Red and Burnt Umber | Purple and Dark Chocolate | Ultra Blue and Burnt Sienna | Kelly Green and Raw Sienna |

Every earth color has its own color family. In bottled acrylics these colors may not be true earth colors, but they can be used in a similar manner. The bottom half of these blocks show the less intense color made by adding an earth color to a primary color.

If you find a color is too bright, try adding more water in your brush or, better yet, don't pick up as much paint in your brush.

A change of intensity can be used to divide and separate. Use an intense color on the edge of a petal the next time you want to separate two petals of equal value. A color's complement can be used to shade in the center of interest area. As you move away from the center of interest, separate values with an earth color. The background color can be used to decrease the intensity of a shading color and help place the flower in the background. Notice how distracting the centers become when intensity is not controlled, even in small areas. The viewer's eye wants to jump between the centers of the two outside blossoms.

Temperature

Temperature is the third element of color theory. Each color has its own temperature. Colors that can be associated with fire or the sun are known as warm colors—of these orange is the warmest. Think of cool colors as those you might see if you were out in space looking down on the earth: the blues of the oceans and the greens of the foliage. The coolest of these colors is blue.

When comparing the relationship of colors to each other, remember each color has a warm and a cool side. For instance, when compared to Bright Red, Maroon is a cooler red and Coral is a warmer red.

I think temperature is one of the most underused characteristics of color in decorative painting. Warm and cool colors can help separate and add depth: warm colors come forward and cool colors recede. Therefore the warmest objects in a painting should be in the front plane or closest to the light source. As objects turn away from the light they become cooler. This change in temperature can be very slight and still lift a petal or set one back.

Temperature can affect an object's position in a painting as warm colors come forward and cool colors recede. You will notice warm colors before you notice cool colors.

The colors in the column on the left are all warmer than those on the right. Even though the yellows, oranges and reds are considered warm colors, you can see that some warm colors are cooler than others; some of the cool violets, blues, greens and neutrals are warmer than others.

Yellow	Bright Yellow
Bittersweet	Orange
Bright Red	Tompte Red
Lilac	Lavender
Blue Wisp	Wedgwood Blue
Leprechaun	Alpine Green
Antique White	Magnolia White
Mudstone	Bridgeport Gray

Using Warm and Cool Colors

When you're looking for variation in your painting, instead of completely changing the color of an object, why not just vary the temperature? Variety is better than same-old same-old. Leaves become more interesting when you have warm, cool and neutral greens. This slight change allows variation, adds interest and yet keeps the painting unified. Remember, keep the changes subtle.

Sometimes when painting flowers, especially cooler petals, the light value becomes too white or too cool, resulting in a dead-looking flower. If this happens, wash the flower or leaf with a warm color.

Poppies and Blossoms Changing the temperature of an object does not necessarily mean a drastic or obvious change. The light flowers have subtle temperature changes helping them establish and maintain their position in the painting. The warmer whites come forward, the cooler whites—to which scant amounts of the cool background color was added—gradually recede.

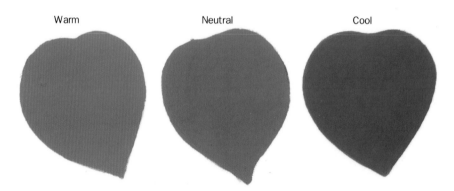

Warm   Neutral   Cool

Often leaves share the same value—not only does this become boring, but as you try to separate them they can look outlined. Varying the temperature of leaves is another option to help separate and add interest.

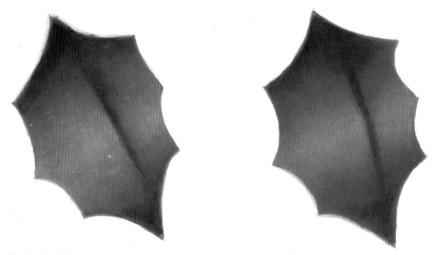

If painting light values causes the object to appear dead, wash it with a warm color, as shown on the right.

*A*ll living things are warm and most are yellow-green—just look at the centers of most flowers. I often use a warm tint to help make a flower come alive. A warm wash also brings the flower forward. A cool wash sets petals or leaves back. When using a wash, keep it very light and repeat if necessary.

You can see the bright yellow-green center on this poppy.

Although smaller than the poppy center, the yellow-green is still visible in this pansy center.

If a flower appears dead or dull, add some yellow to the light values. It not only helps it to look alive, it also helps give the flower petals dimension and movement.

To set a flower or leaf back apply a light wash of a cool color, repeating until it has receded, as on the bottom half of these blocks. A light wash of the cool background color was applied to the large poppy in Poppies And Blossoms on page 42.

We tend to think that white is the best color for a highlight just because it is so light, but in reality white is a cool color. If you want your highlight to have even more of a punch, try adding a touch of warm yellow to your white.

When I think of reflected light, I usually think of a duller or grayer color, but reflected light can be warm, especially if it is bouncing off warm objects. I like to use the object's complement plus a gray mix for reflected light.

Shadows are generally cool in relation to the lighted surface they fall upon, although many shadows do have warm areas reflected in them. Many times I will add a cooler color to my shading value or use a bottled color that is cooler. The gray mix I get when I use the bottled acrylic paint is cool, so I often choose a gray mix to shade.

Because of its temperature, the mix decreases intensity and helps the shaded side recede.

Backgrounds can also be warm or cool. I've often heard that one should use a warm background for a cool design or a cool background for a warm design. On a warm background cool colors come forward and on a cool background warm colors come forward. This works, but can be very distracting if not handled well. A large warm object on a cool background may be all the viewer sees even when the details, values and intensities around it are painted beautifully.

In the painting *Poppies and a Visiting Blue* on page 46, temperature change— along with intensity and value change—make this design come together and work.

Cast shadows anchor an object to a surface and give it stability. Warmer colors can be present in cast shadows—notice the warm pink shadow on the upper edge of this flower. The painting on page 46 also uses warm colors in its cast shadows.

The temperature of a background can affect the position of an object in a painting. On a warm background, cool colors like this blue come forward and warm colors recede. When using this option be sure you also consider the value.

On a cool background, warm objects like this orange come forward and cool objects recede. Again, when considering temperature to convey an object's placement, remember the color's value too.

When there is a vast temperature change between a large object in a design and the background, it can be very distracting. The light warm flowers come forward because of their value and temperature. The large flower is closer in value to the background, but because of its size and temperature in relation to the cool background, the viewer's eye jumps there and stops.

Poppies and a Visiting Blue In this piece the warm orange flowers on the cool blue background are controlled using values, temperatures and intensities. The eye is drawn to the area around the butterfly. This is where the lightest and brightest poppies and warmest colors are located. The poppies become duller, darker and cooler away from the center of interest.

The first step in choosing your shading and light values is to identify the color family of the basecoat color. This circle is in the yellow-orange family and the cylinder is in the red-violet family.

Applying What You've Learned

Now that you understand what different values, intensities and temperatures can do for your painting, your next step is deciding which colors you want to use. The easy part of choosing colors for your painting is when you know you want to basecoat with a light, warm pink—you simply go to your paint supply and pick the color you want. It's the right value, intensity and temperature. Because of recent advancements in the technological world, paint colors have become more consistent from batch to batch—today color computers scan the dye lots for uniformity in color.

The problems arise when you need to shade and highlight that particular color and can't decide which colors to use. I use Delta Ceramcoat Acrylics, but my method for determining a color's characteristics can be used with any brand of paint.

The first thing to ask yourself is what color family do I need? A warm pink for example, would fall into the family of reds.

The next question is, what values do you want? You need anywhere from three to five value changes to create a truly three-dimensional form. For shading, you know you want at least two to three darker values and two to three lighter values for highlights, and you also know the closer in value the colors are the easier it will be to bridge the transition area—maybe you'll use more than two or three dark values. Keep in mind what looks good in a bottle or on a palette may not work on the surface as well as you think—you have to try it on the actual basecoated surface to be sure.

In the top sphere, the first value shade color is very close in value to the basecoat. This makes it easier to carry the shading value out onto the sphere and eliminate any transition line. On the other hand, the cylinder is shaded with a value that is too dark, making it difficult to bridge the transition area. It's also bright and does not relate well to the basecoat color. In the middle sphere, even though the first value shading worked very well, the second value shading is too dark, causing poor value change. The dark value looks almost isolated. The cylinder in the middle example is shaded with a corner of the brush loaded in both the basecoat color and the first value shade color. This not only helps bridge the values, but makes the basecoat and shading values relate better. The result is a smoother, better transition from dark value to middle value. The third example shows a better, more gradual dark value change on both the sphere and the cylinder. The same dark value was used again on the cylinder, but notice how much better it looks because the values are closer and the intensity of the colors has been bridged.

The next question is, what about intensity? Think about what mixing your color with a complementary color, gray, earth tone, or other will do to its intensity. Do you want the object to maintain the intensity of the basecoat color?

What about temperature? Would the cooler side of your basecoat color work best to help your shaded areas recede? Do you need a warmer light to make the light value areas come forward and look alive?

When a color is too dark to determine its temperature or intensity, add white in small amounts and create a value scale. Once the scale is complete, you will probably find that the gradations you have created match up to other bottled colors, giving you a key to what premixed colors you could try as shading colors. Adding a touch of white to your color will also help if you are having problems fitting an earth color into its proper color family. Sometimes when you add white to familiar colors, you may be surprised by the results.

Once you have decided on colors, you may find gaps in value and intensity, or a color may be too warm or cool when compared to the basecoat or previous shade or highlight value. When this occurs, you can bridge the gap to make the two colors relate better by loading both colors in the same corner of your brush at once.

When it is necessary to add a small amount of a cooler, warmer, lighter, darker, brighter or duller color, pick up both colors in your brush and "brush mix" as you paint. This works better than mixing a puddle of paint with a palette knife because you can achieve a more subtle, varied change in the color. Brush mixing helps give variety and prevents a color from becoming boring. Both techniques will be explained in detail in the next chapter.

Candy Bar Brown

Rose Mist

Bouquet Pink

Sachet Pink

Rose Cloud

This value scale was made using Candy Bar Brown and White. As the values become lighter you can identify some bottled colors: Rose Mist, Bouquet Pink, Sachet Pink and Rose Cloud. If you want a more perfect match, add a touch of Bright Red to Rose Mist and Rose Cloud; these are a tiny bit duller than the colors on the value scale.

Dark Chocolate	Walnut	Burnt Umber	Brown Velvet

These four value scales are painted using Dark Chocolate, Walnut, Burnt Umber and Brown Velvet. Once Dark Chocolate is mixed with white, it becomes obvious it is a cooler brown and can be used to dull or shade. Walnut appears cool, yet warmer than Dark Chocolate. It may work if used to shade some of the bottled grays. Burnt Umber is warmer still and may be a good choice for shading with duller reds. Brown Velvet is the warmest of the browns. Shading dull, warmer reds and oranges uses it to its best advantage.

Boston Fern	Dark Jungle Green	Dark Forest Green	English Yew Green

The top row of colors are all darker value greens that work well to shade leaves. When you study the colors with white added, you can make the best choice for position in the design. Boston Fern is the warmest of the greens, so it would work best in the center of interest area. Dark Jungle Green is not as warm, and may work well on a cooler, duller leaf in the center of interest or in the middle plane. Dark Forest Green is a cooler green, a good color to use when you want a color to recede. English Yew Green is duller in relationship to the other greens and would work well to shade a more neutral leaf.

CHAPTER THREE

Practicing Decorative Painting Techniques

Floating Color

I use many different techniques when painting. The more realistic I want the painting to be, the more advanced the techniques I use—like those involving extender. If I have a faster, easier project in mind, I may rely on more traditional techniques like floating color. If I want to create a soft, light mood, I may just use lots of water. No matter which technique you choose, be sure you are comfortable, have good tools and discipline yourself.

Floating color is one of the first techniques decorative painters learn for shading and lightening. In this technique apply color using a damp, flat brush, corner-loaded in paint and dressed on the palette. When you float color, the objective is to leave a darker or lighter value on or along an area without leaving a transition line where the values change, allowing the floated color to gradually melt into the background color.

It may take you several minutes to dress or load your brush to float color. Be willing to spend as much time as it takes.

To successfully float color you will need:
- the right size brush with a good chisel edge
- clean droplets of water on your palette
- paper towel
- clean palette to dress your brush on
- fresh paint

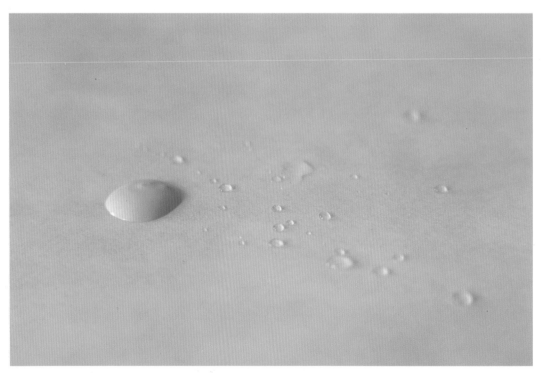

Step 1 Apply a small amount of paint to your palette. Rinse your brush and splatter some droplets of clean water on your palette. Now blot your brush on a paper towel, making sure there are no droplets ready to run off the ferrule of the brush. Dip the corner of your brush in these water droplets anytime you need to pick up extra water for floating color. This way you control the amount of water in your brush.

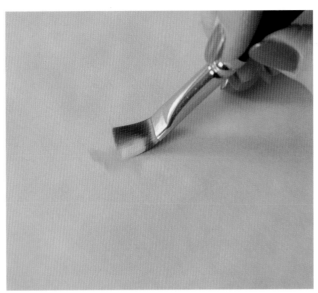

Step 2 Touch the corner of your brush into the paint, picking up a very small amount. When you corner load your brush, make sure only the corner enters the paint. Don't tip your brush or you'll pick up paint along an entire edge.

Step 3 Work the paint into your brush gradually by applying pressure and pulling short, straight strokes one on top of the other. Try to confine the area on your palette where you dress your brush to no more than ½" (1.3cm) to ¾" (1.9cm).

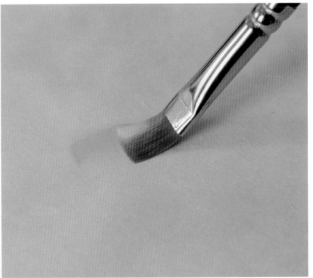

Step 4 If the paint is not working far enough into the brush, try "walking" the brush sideways into the area where you've been pulling your strokes and back out. Walk the paint-filled side of your brush in as far as you can and still leave the opposite edge clean. Be sure you pick the paint back up in your brush as you move out. If you're still having difficulty getting the paint worked into your brush, apply pressure and squiggle the brush.

Step 5 It's necessary to dress both sides of your brush to prevent globs of paint from gathering on one side. You can either move back and forth with the brush or flip the brush to the other side. If you flip the brush be sure you overlap the paint already on the palette, leaving one side clean, and that you pick the paint up as you leave the palette.

Wrong way. When you use long strokes to dress your brush you leave the paint on the palette, not in the brush. For the same reason, avoid moving all over your palette as you dress your brush.

Step 6 Water is necessary to transport the paint out of your brush. If you don't have enough water you may not be able to float the color as far as you would like, or you may end up with a dry brush look. As you pick up a little more paint on the paint-filled corner, touch the opposite corner in a tiny droplet of water. If you touch your brush in the basin, you pick up so much water, it is hard to maintain a clean edge.

Step 7 Continue dressing the brush as described above, using the same area of your palette. Repeat the previous steps as many times as necessary until your brush contains not only enough paint but also enough water to get you where you want to go. At this point the paint should be two-thirds to three-fourths of the way across the bottom of the brush. When you apply pressure you should see a triangle of color. You are now ready to float the color onto the basecoated surface.

Step 8 Keep your brush flat when you float color, maintaining equal pressure across the hairs. If you're painting with the corner of your brush, you may end up with a stripe of color rather than a smooth gradation. Be sure you're applying enough pressure on the brush to release the paint and water.

It's inevitable: You will occasionally have a water or drying line appear on the clean edge of the float. Quickly take a clean, damp brush and lightly touch the line to remove it. Remember, the closer in value the floated color is to the basecoat color, the easier it is to avoid an apparent transition line.

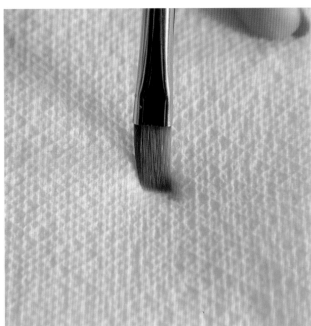

If your floating color disappears and you are using the same color, don't rinse your brush—chances are you ran out of water, not paint. Simply reload and redress your brush using droplets of water and tiny corner loads of paint. If it's necessary to change colors, rinse your brush well. When you reload your brush, always reload the same corner of the brush in the paint. If you don't, eventually a dirty water line will appear as you paint. To check which corner of the brush was previously loaded with paint, blot the brush on a paper towel. Some residual paint from the corner used should be evident, especially near the ferrule.

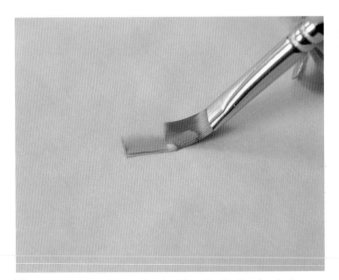

When you want to use two colors together, load both colors in the same corner of your brush. Add only a small amount of each color. Then load and dress the brush as previously described for floating color. Adjust the colors as you load the brush.

Pitfalls to avoid when floating color:
- brush with no chisel edge
- the wrong size brush
- too little water
- too much paint at once into your brush
- not dressing your brush on both sides
- using too large an area of your palette to dress your brush
- leaving all the paint on your palette

Wet in Wet

Painting wet in wet is another technique I use. This simply means to apply paint to your surface and, while it is still wet, blend it with wet paint from your brush. You have to work a little more quickly than you do when painting on a dry surface, but this does create a smooth, gradual transition of values.

Step 1 Paint the dark value area using a heavy amount of paint. You want this area to stay wet while you apply the next value.

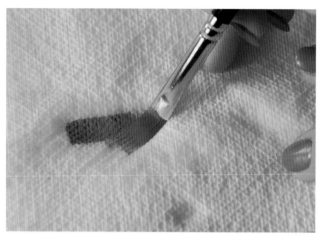

Step 2 Quickly dry wipe your brush in a damp area of your paper towel to remove most of the paint—don't rinse it out. This will give you what is called a "dirty brush."

Step 3 Before the dark value has a chance to dry, pick up the light value with your dirty brush. Fill in the light value area, then begin to work the light value paint into the dark value, blending and softening as you stroke the colors together. Once you have picked up some of the darker value in your brush don't go back and contaminate the light value.

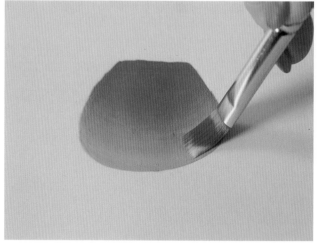

Step 4 If you need to keep blending, dry wipe the paint out of the brush. Continue softening and blending until there is a gradual value change from light to dark. To obtain a little more blending time, touch the corner of the brush into a small droplet of water. Stop once the paint has started to set or dry.

*I*f I'm painting a larger area, like an entire background, I usually apply a generous amount of paint and carry more water in my brush. I may also dampen the surface before I begin. If I want the background to have several muted colors visible, I may scumble it in using wet paint.

Step 1 Apply random strokes of heavy color with a large brush. It's always good to include a neutral or resting color. Don't be concerned if there are a few blank spaces between strokes.

Step 2 Dry wipe your brush in a paper towel and begin to soften the strokes of color using short, quick strokes in all directions. Dry wipe excess paint out of your brush as you continue to soften.

Step 3 Continue to soften and blend colors. You can leave obvious brush strokes or continue until the brush strokes are light. Don't overblend—you should be able to identify each of the colors in some areas.

Extender

When I paint more detailed designs, I tend to use extender—a medium that retards the drying time of acrylic paint for three to five minutes. This allows me more time to blend and soften the paint. Depending on the brush I use, extender can create several different effects.

Select a brush to apply the extender you won't be using during the painting session. You don't want to rinse your extender brush before using it because water will dilute the retarding properties—extender won't dry in your brush or cause any damage if left in during the painting session. After you're done painting, clean your brush in the usual manner.

I never use a stay-wet palette when I'm using extender because I feel it also dilutes the extending properties. Water will remove paint mixed with extender for about twenty to thirty minutes after it has been applied.

Begin by brushing a thin coat of extender on the surface. It doesn't matter if the extender goes beyond the basecoated design area. When you tilt the surface you want to see an even sheen with no brush marks, runs or dry, spotty areas. If a halo forms when you apply the paint, you are unable to control the paint, or you aren't leaving any paint on the surface the extender is too wet. If this happens, blot your extender brush on your paper towel, brush over the surface and blot again.

If your paint grabs when applied, the extender is too dry and needs to be reapplied. The paint that grabbed will reactivate and melt with the fresh application of extender. The next value may be applied over the same application of extender as long as it is still wet.

If the area starts to set, stop immediately. If you continue you risk lifting paint. If you are uncertain whether the area is dry enough to reapply extender, begin to reapply very carefully and stop if you feel you are removing paint. The painted areas may be dry enough to reapply extender even if the surrounding surface appears to be wet.

Depending on the difference in values or even the amount of time you work in a certain area, the paint may begin to look blotchy or uneven. Stop when this happens, don't continue to overwork it. Let the area dry and repeat the step. It will even out with the next application of paint.

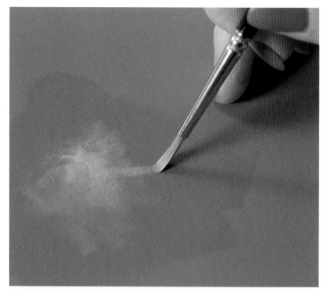

If the extender is too wet, the paint will bleed and a halo of paint will spread into unwanted areas.

If you are unsure whether the paint is dry enough to carefully reapply a small area with extender, stroke over the area with extender, then blot your brush on a paper towel. If no color is visible it is safe to continue.

Stop blending and allow the paint to dry if the application of a darker or lighter value appears spotty or blotchy.

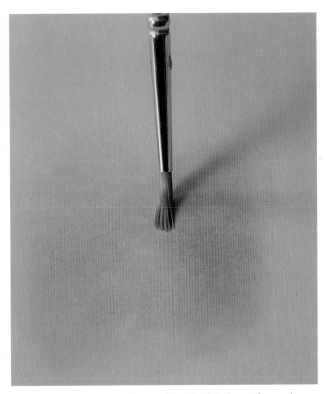

When the area is dry, reapply extender and paint, then soften and blend. The blotchiness should disappear.

Flat Brush

Use a flat brush when you want to shade or lighten along an edge. Rinse your brush and blot it firmly on your paper towel. Corner load the brush and dress it on your palette as you do when floating color. It isn't critical that you keep one edge color free.

Apply the paint in a pat and pull motion. If you apply the paint in long continuous strokes as you do when floating color, the paint will begin to move and collect along the outside edge, causing a ridge. If a ridge sets, touch an old scruffy brush in a small amount of extender and gently scrub into the ridge causing it to blend and soften into the background—if you are too firm, you may dig into the surface.

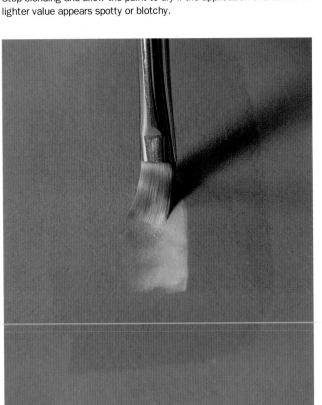

Apply paint in a pat and pull motion. You don't have to maintain an even edge as you will be pulling and blending the paint.

Once the paint is applied, dry wipe excess paint out of your brush in a damp area of your paper towel.

Gently pull color onto the surface until it fades into the background. Soften the background with feather-light overstrokes on the inside edge. If you feel you are picking up too much color and carrying it farther than desired, dry wipe the brush in your paper towel and continue to blend and soften. If you rinse your brush and try to soften with a damp brush, you will remove paint.

If you are used to floating color, you may have a tendency to apply the paint in long, even strokes. If you continue to stroke over the area, the paint will eventually work its way to the outside edge and create an unwanted ridge.

If you happen to create a ridge, load a small scruffy brush in a drop of extender and gently work into the ridge. It should melt the ridge and the reactivated paint can be softened and blended into the background. After paint has been applied, be sure to dry wipe your brush in a damp area of your paper towel to remove the excess paint.

Begin pulling paint from the edge with your flat brush. Be sure you bring the paint out as far as necessary to create good form. Once you have pulled the paint out, gently soften the interior edge with feather-light strokes.

Round Brush

When painting light values on spheres, use a round brush loaded in your light value color. Brush on extender and apply paint in an irregular star shape. Dry wipe your brush in a damp area of your paper towel and flatten. Begin softening color around the outside edge, turning your piece and pulling color onto the surface in all directions. Once the edge is softened and blended, soften the center using feather-light strokes.

To paint the light value on a cylinder-type petal or leaf, apply extender to the area and load a round brush in your light value. Apply paint in a narrow line in the light value area.

To soften a narrow line, outline or edge, straddle the paint and stroke over the line until it's softened into the background.

Light values in a sphere or globular shaped flower are painted using a round brush. Apply the paint in an irregular star shape.

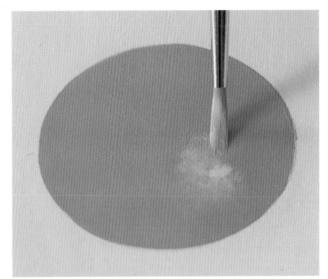

Dry wipe your brush in a damp area of your paper towel, flattening the bristles as you remove the paint. Begin softening the paint on the outside edge, pulling out onto the surface. Be sure to turn your piece as you blend to maintain good form. If the paint travels onto an area you don't want it in, use a soft scruffy brush to push it in, as shown on page 62.

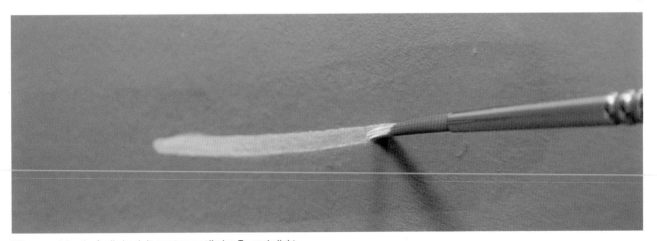

When a petal or leaf rolls back it creates a cylinder. To apply light value to that area, load and dress a round brush in the light value and apply it in a solid line to the light value area.

Soft Scruffy Brush

Often when you are shading or lightening, the paint travels beyond where you want it. When this happens, bring the paint back into the desired area with a dry soft scruffy brush, dry wiping in a damp area of your paper towel as you pick up excess paint.

Use an old, soft scruffy brush that will straddle the light value line.

Stroke back and forth over the light value until the paint has blended into the background. If the light value continues to look like a stripe, apply more pressure to your brush and gently move the brush side to side as you move back and forth.

Round Sable Brush

You may try softening edges with a short round sable brush. This brush tends to remove paint and extender, along with softening the edges, making it necessary to repeat paint application. Always try softening and blending with the brush you applied paint with first.

Use a short round sable to soften edges, or to bring your paint back into a desired area. This brush also works well to blend and soften areas where the paint is just starting to set. Because it removes a fair amount of paint when used for blending, I would reserve it for areas that are difficult to soften with the softer synthetic brushes. Dry wipe paint and extender out of the brush on a damp area of a paper towel. Don't rinse the brush.

Liner Brush

At times it is necessary to darken small triangles or the small dark areas under petal ruffles. To do this, have a few drops of extender on your palette and touch a no. 2 liner brush into the extender and then into the paint. This is the only time I use extender in the painting brush. Fill in the small areas. Dry wipe the brush on a damp area of your paper towel, flattening the brush as you do so. Begin to gently soften the outside edge only—don't work into the darkest area. Dry wipe your brush as you pick up excess paint.

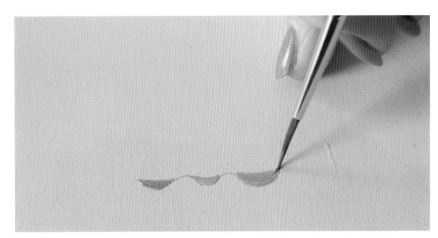

When it is necessary to shade in small areas, use a no. 2 liner loaded in a small amount of paint and a drop of extender.

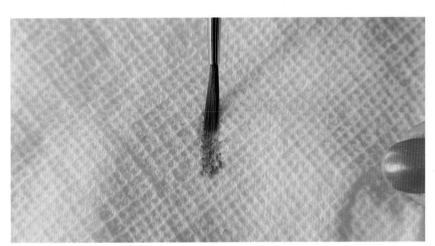

As you remove excess paint from your brush in the damp area of your paper towel, flatten the liner to resemble a small flat.

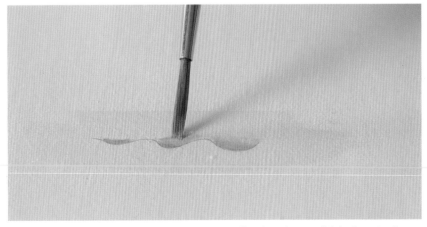

Using the flattened liner, begin to soften the edge, pulling the paint out slightly. Do not pull paint out from the inside edge or corner. Avoid a stiff, outlined look caused by a continuous dark value around the edges of petals. If your area does appear outlined, work into the dark line to remove it. Use this technique to make untidy edges clean and crisp.

Washes

Painting with washes of color is another technique I use when I want a soft look, especially for backgrounds. I often paint leaves starting with washes.

The most important thing to remember when painting with washes is to mix enough wash initially. Otherwise, you'll be stopping in the middle of your application to mix more wash, and, before you know it, you're struggling to remove drying lines. If you know you want to cover a large surface, mix your wash in a small container; for smaller areas a bubble palette works well.

I generally separate and identify washes by their consistency or opacity. A light wash is transparent. You can see the background through it and it doesn't really change the color of the background. You might use a light wash to warm a petal or cool a leaf.

A medium wash consistency is slightly opaque—you can see the background, but the color is stronger. I would use a medium wash to create a stained background look.

A heavy wash is almost opaque. It may be used to paint an entire background, or just to darken the edges.

When I want to mix a small puddle for a wash, I generally brush mix the water and paint on my palette. If I need a larger quantity, I may use an old liner brush to mix the water and paint in a separate container. Once you have

A light wash will appear transparent.

A heavy wash will appear almost opaque.

A medium wash will still be transparent, but the color will be obvious.

made your wash, rinse your brush and blot it firmly on your paper towel. Pick up a small amount of wash in your brush and quickly blot again before application.

If you are unsuccessful with applications of washes because they are too heavy, uneven or blotchy, it is because you had too much water and paint in your brush to begin with. You may find it hard to control the wash when painting along the edges of objects, and you might develop overlaps. Remember, you can always repeat a wash that is too light, but it's next to impossible to remove too much paint.

At times I have wanted to cool a leaf, lose an edge or set an entire object into the background so I painted the area with a wash consistency. Begin painting where you want your color the strongest; as you move away the color will become weaker and weaker until you can no longer see a value or color change.

Blot your brush well before picking up the wash. Touch into the wash to pick up the paint and water mix.

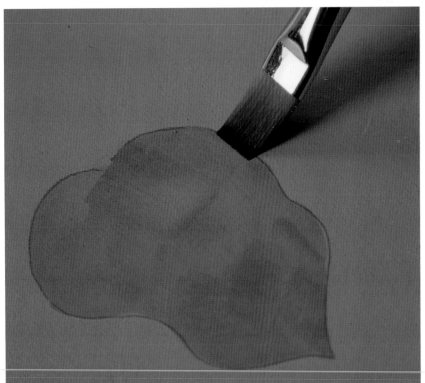

Begin applying the wash where you want the strongest color and work out until the wash is no longer apparent.

A brush that is overloaded with paint and water will cause overlaps and uneven coverage. Blot your brush on the damp area of your paper towel until there is an even release of wash from your brush.

Wet Brush

For many of my smaller paintings, I use what I call a wet brush technique. I carry the paint out onto the surface using a very wet brush, a tiny amount of paint and lots of pressure. This technique requires several applications of paint—with many of the same values repeated two to three times—but because the water and paint dry rapidly you can move around your piece at a nice pace.

Begin by loading the corner of a very damp brush in a pinhead of paint. Dress on palette.

As you apply pressure, water and a small amount of color are released from your brush. Let the water carry the paint onto the surface. As you set the brush down, apply pressure to release enough water to continue moving out onto your object until there is no pigment left.

Because the water precedes the paint on the surface, the paint will melt in to the background, usually without any drying line. If a drying line does occur, just touch it with a clean damp brush. It will melt away.

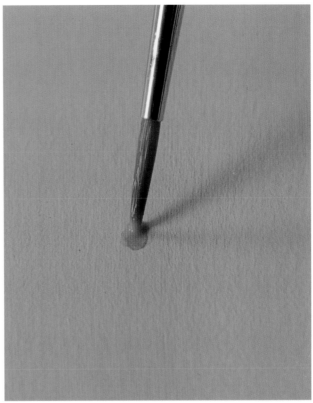

The light value area is applied using a damp round or liner brush loaded with a scant amount of paint. Touch down on the surface, releasing paint and water.

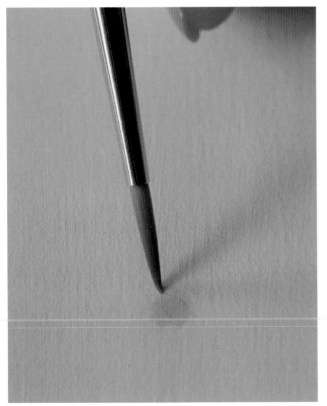

To get rid of drying lines, rinse your brush, then touch the damp brush to the outside edge, scooting paint and water into the background.

CHAPTER FOUR

Painting Realistic Flowers

Tips for Success

*B*efore you begin to paint individual flowers or floral designs I want to share some of the tips I've come up with over the years—perhaps you will avoid a few pitfalls and be more pleased with your finished work.

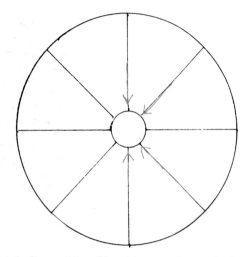

All Petals Connect to a Stem It's easy to lose track when painting a multipetaled flower, like a rose. Before you know it, you have painted all these beautiful petals, and the center no longer appears to connect to the stem. This may give it an unnatural position, making the center appear to be sitting off to the side. A flower can also appear lopsided when you paint more petals on one side. It's important to paint each petal as if you were connecting it to the stem, even if the stem isn't visible. This helps maintain the proper appearance of the flower. When you paint ruffles or rolls in petals, think of them as spokes in a wagon wheel—they should all point in to the center, or axle. Small, sharp ruffles along the edge of a petal are the exception. These do not necessarily have to appear to follow through to the center.

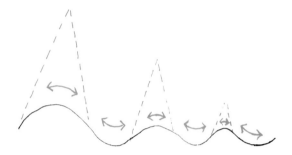

Vary Your Petals If you have a flower that has many ruffles or rolls, like a pansy or sweet pea, be sure you vary the width, length and value of each. Keep the roll directed toward the center as it narrows.

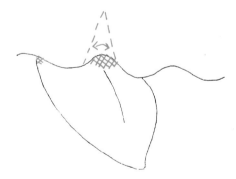

Lift With Dark Values If you are going to paint one petal on top of another, first consider the light source. It's much easier to separate or lift a petal if you can tuck dark value under light values. I wouldn't recommend painting every petal dark under the left and light to the right, but if you want one individual petal to lift, look for an area where shadows can fall.

Determine the Basic Shapes of the Flower

Before you start painting a flower, you should determine whether the whole flower is one basic shape or more. Once you do this, you know where the darkest and lightest petals fall.

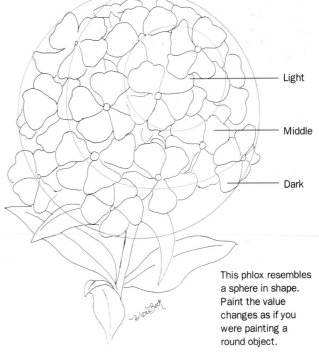

The daffodil contains many cylinders. The cup of the daffodil itself is a cylinder. As this rolls out it also forms a partial cylinder. When the petals grow out and tip down, they are painted with the same value changes that occur when painting a cylinder.

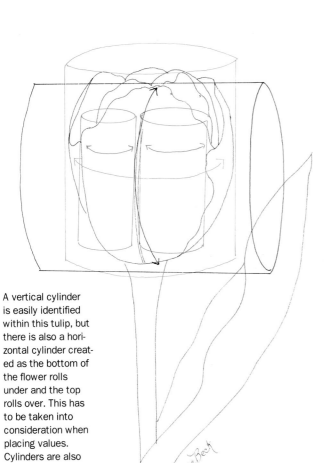

A vertical cylinder is easily identified within this tulip, but there is also a horizontal cylinder created as the bottom of the flower rolls under and the top rolls over. This has to be taken into consideration when placing values. Cylinders are also created as the center petal rolls away from the edges and toward the vein line.

Light

Middle

Dark

This phlox resembles a sphere in shape. Paint the value changes as if you were painting a round object.

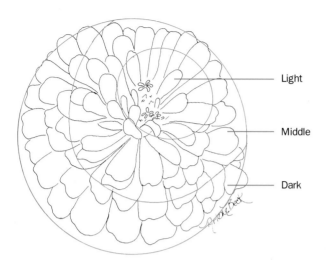

Light

Middle

Dark

As the zinnia blossom opens, it too resembles a sphere. The darkest petals fall in the dark value area, the lightest petals fall in the light value area.

Light

Middle

Dark

The foxglove is shaped like a cone or triangle. The individual blossoms are also cone shaped.

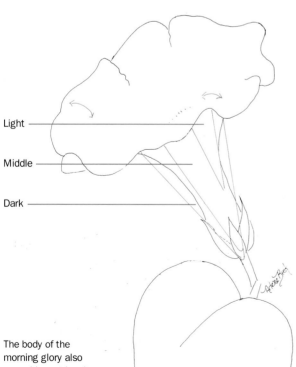

Light

Middle

Dark

The body of the morning glory also resembles a triangle before opening and rolling out to form cylinder shapes.

Identify Combinations of Shapes

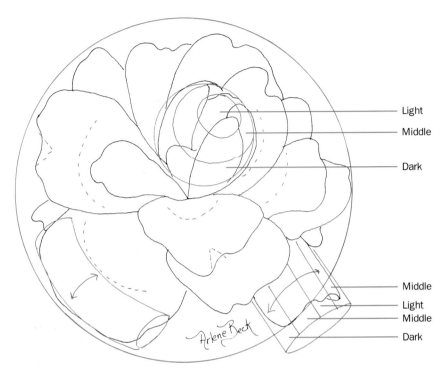

— Light
— Middle

— Dark

— Middle
— Light
— Middle
— Dark

The rose itself is a sphere. The unopened center is also a sphere. Cylinders can be identified in rolling petals and triangles seen where they ruffle.

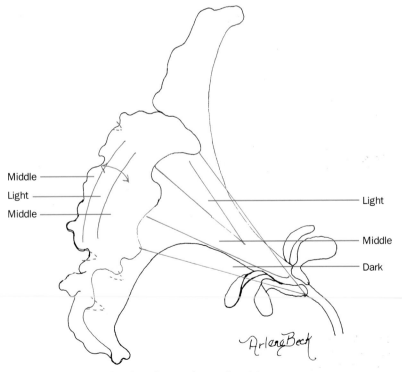

Middle —
Light —
Middle —

— Light

— Middle

— Dark

This side view of a petunia contains a triangle, cylinders where it rolls out and triangles on the frilled outside edges.

Identify Basic Shapes in the Smaller Details

Once you determine the basic shape, you can move on to different sections of the flower, to individual petals and finally to specific details on the petals. As petals roll, fold, cup, ruffle, bend or curve, different shapes can be identified. The type of flower, petal and how fully the blossom is opened also determine the different shapes found in petals. As I mentioned before, it may be easiest to enlarge the flower and take it apart petal by petal to identify the different shapes. An upper right center light source is used with all these examples.

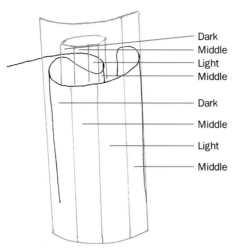

This petal rolls and folds upon itself several times; therefore it has many cylinders. Even though the back edge of the large roll touches the rest of the petal, there has to be value change as the roll creates a cylinder. Don't submit to the temptation of putting light value on the edge of the roll. Always think value placement to create form first. As the petal rolls back upon itself it creates another cylinder, which also has to be painted with proper value change.

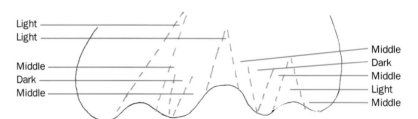

Rolling edges on petals follow the shape of triangles. The lightest area occurs where the petal rolls up and the darkest area as the roll dips.

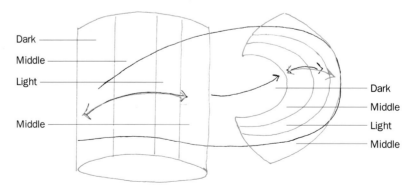

This zinnia petal is an example of a cupped petal. It resembles three different cylinders: first as it rolls out and up from the center, second as it rolls down creating the cup and finally as it creates the rolling top portion of the petal.

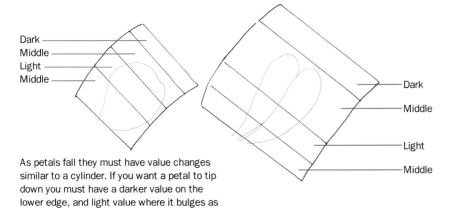

Dark
Middle
Light
Middle

Dark

Middle

Light

Middle

As petals fall they must have value changes similar to a cylinder. If you want a petal to tip down you must have a darker value on the lower edge, and light value where it bulges as it bends.

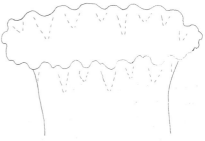

The edges of many flowers are frilled or ruffled. Each or these tiny ruffles must have value change resembling small triangles or cones. Remember, small ruffles do not have to follow through to the center.

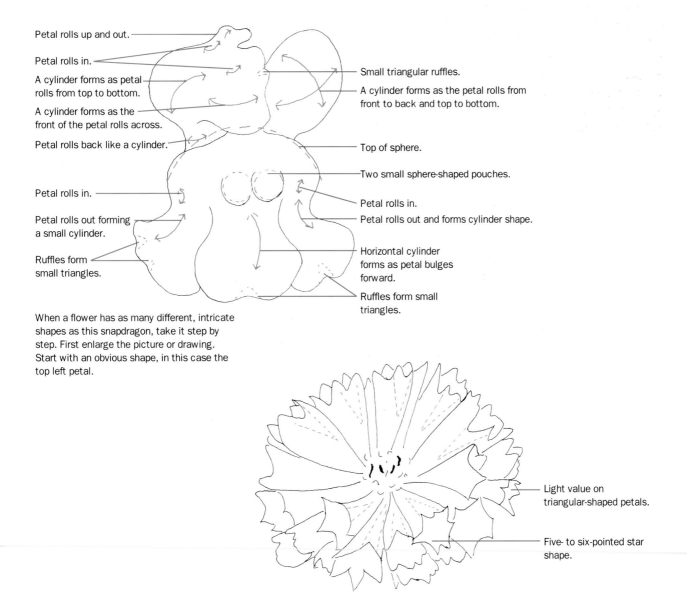

Petal rolls up and out.

Petal rolls in.

A cylinder forms as petal rolls from top to bottom.

A cylinder forms as the front of the petal rolls across.

Petal rolls back like a cylinder.

Petal rolls in.

Petal rolls out forming a small cylinder.

Ruffles form small triangles.

Small triangular ruffles.

A cylinder forms as the petal rolls from front to back and top to bottom.

Top of sphere.

Two small sphere-shaped pouches.

Petal rolls in.

Petal rolls out and forms cylinder shape.

Horizontal cylinder forms as petal bulges forward.

Ruffles form small triangles.

When a flower has as many different, intricate shapes as this snapdragon, take it step by step. First enlarge the picture or drawing. Start with an obvious shape, in this case the top left petal.

Light value on triangular-shaped petals.

Five- to six-pointed star shape.

When you first look at a cornflower or bachelor's button, the tendency may be to paint a loose, fluffy flower. If you like detail, be willing to take it apart and identify the separate petals. The petals are small and triangular shaped, and end with a jagged star shape with five to six points.

We've already identified the major cylinders in the daffodil. The top edge of the cup ruffles as it rolls out. The values on these triangle ruffles change as the value of the cylinder changes. The petals may roll in from the side edges. If this happens, treat the petal as a vertical cylinder and paint the curled edges as cylinders.

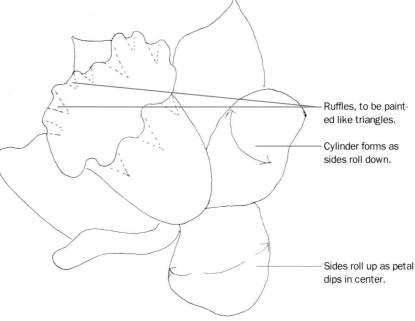

Ruffles, to be painted like triangles.

Cylinder forms as sides roll down.

Sides roll up as petal dips in center.

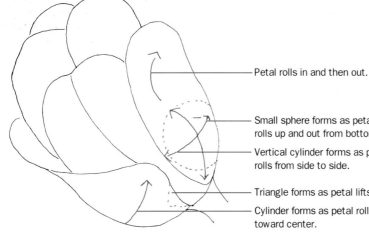

Petal rolls in and then out.

Small sphere forms as petal rolls up and out from bottom.

Vertical cylinder forms as petal rolls from side to side.

Triangle forms as petal lifts up.

Cylinder forms as petal rolls toward center.

The tulip has the value placement of a cylinder. Using an upper right center light source, the light values are placed to the right of center and the dark values are placed to the left. The petal on the right side of this flower creates a vertical cylinder and a small round bulge as it rolls out from the bottom, continuing to roll in and out.

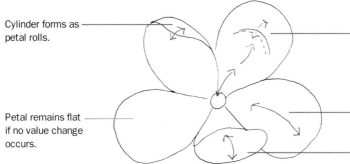

Cylinder forms as petal rolls.

Three cylinders result as this petal rolls out from center of flower, cups in the middle, and rolls out and over.

Cylinder forms as petal bends down.

Petal remains flat if no value change occurs.

Cylinder forms as petal flips up.

In multipetaled flowers, individual petals can curve, bend or cup as shown in this drawing. Paint the flipped areas on the petals as cylinders. Place the values on the cupped petal like three cylinders as it rolls out of the center into the cupped area, then out and rolling back.

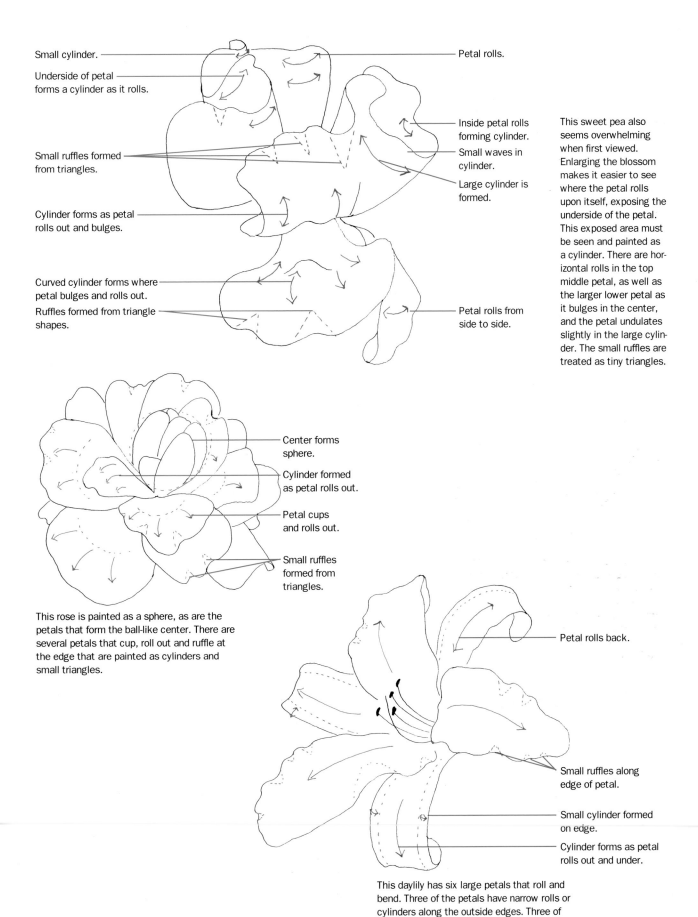

Small cylinder.

Underside of petal forms a cylinder as it rolls.

Small ruffles formed from triangles.

Cylinder forms as petal rolls out and bulges.

Curved cylinder forms where petal bulges and rolls out.

Ruffles formed from triangle shapes.

Petal rolls.

Inside petal rolls forming cylinder.

Small waves in cylinder.

Large cylinder is formed.

Petal rolls from side to side.

This sweet pea also seems overwhelming when first viewed. Enlarging the blossom makes it easier to see where the petal rolls upon itself, exposing the underside of the petal. This exposed area must be seen and painted as a cylinder. There are horizontal rolls in the top middle petal, as well as the larger lower petal as it bulges in the center, and the petal undulates slightly in the large cylinder. The small ruffles are treated as tiny triangles.

Center forms sphere.

Cylinder formed as petal rolls out.

Petal cups and rolls out.

Small ruffles formed from triangles.

This rose is painted as a sphere, as are the petals that form the ball-like center. There are several petals that cup, roll out and ruffle at the edge that are painted as cylinders and small triangles.

Petal rolls back.

Small ruffles along edge of petal.

Small cylinder formed on edge.

Cylinder forms as petal rolls out and under.

This daylily has six large petals that roll and bend. Three of the petals have narrow rolls or cylinders along the outside edges. Three of the petals have frills or short ruffles along their edges and are painted as tiny triangles.

Detailing Flower Centers

Once you have painted your flowers with good value placement, intensity, and temperature control, you are ready to add the details that make the design real. The center is one of the most important details in a flower. The centers of most flowers are different in appearance but contain the same basic parts. The flower is attached to the stem by a small stalk known as the pedicel. The petals are protected by sepals—the tiny, usually green, petals at the base of the flower. Together these sepals make up the calyx. Inside the petals are the stamens, which consist of a filament and anther. The anther is where pollen can be seen. In the center of the stamen is the pistil, consisting of a stigma and a style. The stigma collects pollen.

The larger the stamen and pistils, in lilies and tulips for example, the more important it becomes to see them as basic shapes and treat them with proper value, intensity and temperature control.

How open the petals are and the angle from which the flower is viewed determines the amount of detail in the center of a flower. Often there are multiple stamens, for example in a rose or poppy, surrounding the yellow-green center. Although the centers of flowers are generally bright and warm, the value and intensity of these stamens have to be controlled with their position and design, or the viewer's eye may jump around the painting from one flower's center to another.

There is lots of texture in the centers of flowers. The pistil may have a sticky, wet appearance, while the pollen has a soft, dusty texture. Pollen can often be seen on the pistil and on the petals around the center. Some flowers also have fine hairs that catch pollen, making the center appear to glow with a yellow halo. An example is the yellow comma strokes on pansy centers.

If a center is in full view, the stamens basically appear equal around the center. When a flower is tipped toward you, allow for foreshortening—some of the filaments may not be visible at all. If a center is large, just a few anthers may be visible behind the center. In some cases, you may choose not to show the center at all.

It can add interest and variety to a painting when a flower is facing away from the viewer. It becomes necessary to visualize how it grows from behind or underneath. Flowers facing away will expose interesting stems and calyx.

Some stamens and pistils are fragile and can be indicated by delicate line work, as seen here. To paint these stamens, I start by creating the anthers with small touches of paint around the center, making sure I keep them loose and randomly placed. I change value as I move into shaded areas or on the center itself. I then connect some, but not all of them, to the filament using irregular, loose, fine line work.

The pistils and stamens in these Lewisia are tiny and can be painted with fine line work.

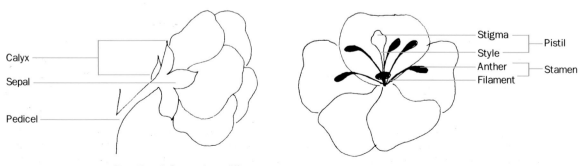

Even though flowers have different appearances they all contain the same basic parts.

Middle
Light
Middle
Dark

Dark
Middle
Light

The centers of flowers are made up of basic shapes. The daisy center rolls out and over creating a cylinder, while the cone flower center resembles a triangle. Be sure petals attach to the body of the center.

Stigma is painted like a sphere.

Value change should be apparent on filament.

Anthers roll like a cylinder.

Stigma rounds and should be painted as top of a sphere.

Anthers and filament roll like a cylinder.

As you choose the colors and values for the pistils and stigmas be sure they relate to the flower and its position in the design.

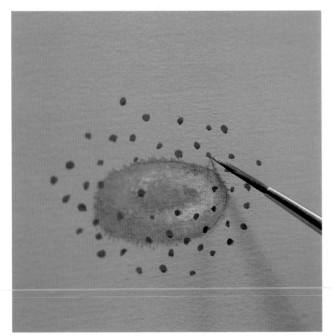

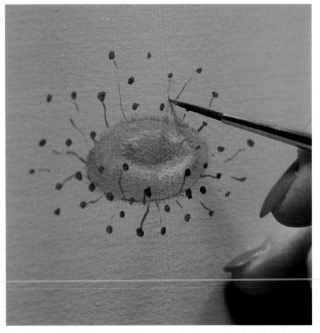

Stipple center using a small scruffy brush. Paint the anthers using a liner brush. Control the intensity and values by brush mixing colors from your palette. Stamens from the front and side of the center can fall on the center, but stamens from the back look peculiar if painted on the center. Avoid placing these more than halfway up the center.

The filament, which connects the anther to the center, is painted using a loose, almost wiggly line. Don't paint a stamen over the entire face of the center. Some of the filaments in the front will look foreshortened while the back may appear longer.

Flower Buds

As every flower is different, so is every bud. Buds can make a design lighter and give it a looser feeling. They also work well as filler flowers. Buds can be an identifying characteristic of a flower—iris and rosebuds are instantly recognizable—so be prepared to paint them well.

Paint buds with basic shapes in mind first, then add the detail. When deciding how much detail to add, be sure to keep the bud's location in the painting in mind—if it isn't near the center of interest, detail should be minimal.

Think green when painting buds, with some of the petal colors present. These small balloon flower buds are painted with proper value change to create their unusual form. Compare these buds to the fully-opened flowers on page 100, the detail here is interesting but it doesn't rival the main flowers.

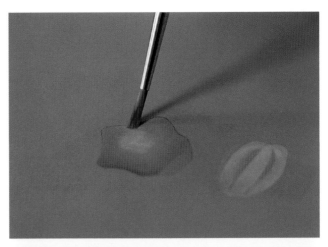

Balloon flower bud.

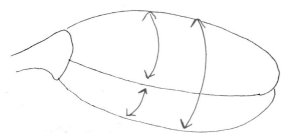

Multiple shapes will be apparent in some buds. This lily bud should be treated as one large cylinder with two small cylinders inside.

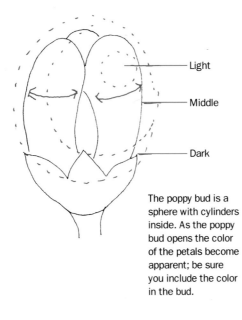

Light

Middle

Dark

The poppy bud is a sphere with cylinders inside. As the poppy bud opens the color of the petals become apparent; be sure you include the color in the bud.

Creating Interest With Light and Shadow

If your subject is sitting in strong light, many petals may change value and color as the light passes through. Reflected light is also obvious on many flowers. Areas of reflected light can help separate petals and provide interest to a painting.

Shadows are another way to make flowers interesting, lending dimension and airiness. To lift a petal up, paint a strong cast shadow. When painting cast shadows, many beginners have a tendency to surround a petal or leaf with dark value. However, light travels in a straight line, and when coming from an upper source it will not cause a shadow behind the entire petal, but will actually travel behind the top of the petal. If there is shading, it is usually there to help push a roll forward, and should not go above the level of the petal.

Light traveling through petals affects their value and colors. Be prepared to add warmer, lighter colors to these areas.

The cast shadows on this zinnia help make the flower appear looser, giving the petals more dimension. The strong shadows lift the top petals off the lower petals. Avoid narrow dark lines under petals; this can make your flower appear stiff and outlined.

In this picture you can see interesting veins and growth lines as the light passes through the petals. Some interesting shadows are also created.

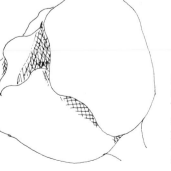

Don't overlook the cast shadow area inside the blossom. The inside petals are tucked down with darker values, but you can make them more interesting by adding a cast shadow on top.

I find most of my students are able to paint cast shadows on leaves without any problem, but forget about those cast within the flower itself. These shadows are important because they will help create the illusion of a turned or tipped petal. Here are a few tips to remember when painting cast shadows within a flower:

• A shadow that separates two petals with a thin dark line can make a flower stiff, while a larger, more realistic shadow will give the illusion of space between the petals.

• Stamens and pistils also cast interesting shadows.

• A shadow follows the contour of the object it falls on.

• Keep shadows duller and darker than the flower.

• Keep shadows transparent.

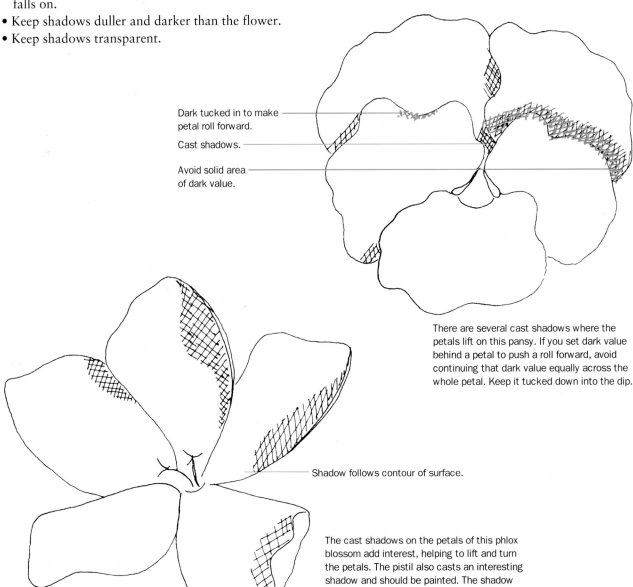

Dark tucked in to make petal roll forward.

Cast shadows.

Avoid solid area of dark value.

There are several cast shadows where the petals lift on this pansy. If you set dark value behind a petal to push a roll forward, avoid continuing that dark value equally across the whole petal. Keep it tucked down into the dip.

Shadow follows contour of surface.

The cast shadows on the petals of this phlox blossom add interest, helping to lift and turn the petals. The pistil also casts an interesting shadow and should be painted. The shadow rolls onto the left petal because shadows follow the contour of the surface they fall on.

Veins in Petals

Many flowers have visible vein lines, others have what I think of as growth lines. Certain pansies would look unfinished if painted without the line work or face. Tulips and violets also have distinctive growth lines. Cosmos and daisies have tiny ridges on their petals. The location of these flowers in your design determines how visible vein details should be.

Dewdrops

Dewdrops are another interesting detail to add to flowers. Dewdrops can help draw a viewer's eye and lead it to another object. Because dewdrops attract attention, keep them close to the center of interest.

The positions of dewdrops have to make sense. If they're sitting on a flat surface, they should have a flat bottom. If they're suspended on a surface which is tipping downward, they must appear to be rolling off in a logical direction. Some other tips about dewdrops:

- Like any other object, dewdrops need value change.
- They cast a shadow onto the surface they sit on.
- They reflect light.
- They are transparent—colors underneath the dewdrop should show through.

To create realistic dewdrops, you need to first study water droplets in an area where there is only one light source—the best place is on a shower wall. You can also sprinkle droplets on a countertop to study the sparkles and shadows.

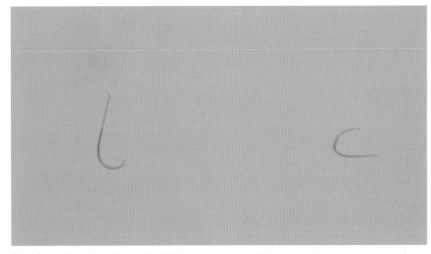

Dewdrops Start by pulling a thin fishhook shape for a rolling drop and an elongated "C" shape for a droplet with a value that is two to three times darker than the value it is resting on. Ask yourself if the drop would be able to continue to roll when placed on a particular petal.

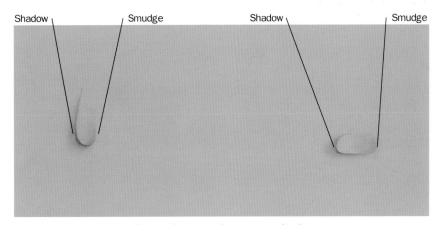

Shadow Smudge Shadow Smudge

Apply extender to the area. Paint a shadow on the area opposite the light source. Using a liner brush dressed in that same dark value, apply the paint, dry wipe, flatten your brush and soften. Paint a soft smudge of dark value where the light will hit the drop.

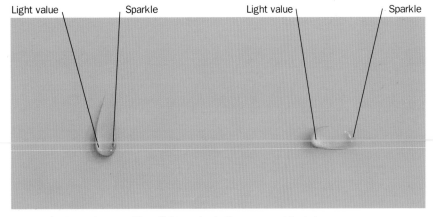

Light value Sparkle Light value Sparkle

Apply extender to the area. Place lighter value in the curve next to, but not on top of, the shadow. Dry wipe, flatten your brush and soften. When dry, add sparkle and a tiny dash where the light hits the drop.

Tints and Accents

I remember being told to think of tints and accents as little bugs that hop through a painting, leaving color wherever they light. More literally, a tint is any color with white or a lighter value added to it. An accent is any color used to help unify a painting.

Accents, which I think of as strong or almost pure color, play an important role in carrying color throughout a painting. Accents are always colors you have already used elsewhere in your painting, although you can dull, darken or lighten them as needed. Use accents to help balance a painting—if you have a strong color or large area of one color in part of the painting, repeat it as an accent throughout the rest of the painting. You can also use tints and accents to carry flower color onto leaves and into shadows. Darker or cooler accents can help turn a petal back or make it tip down.

Make sure your strongest tints and accents fall in the center of interest area. If I'm unsure about an area being too light or bright, I start in the center of interest and pick out the area I want to have the lightest or brightest tint. I then work outward from that area, making sure each following tint or accent is duller or darker than the last.

Always place tints and accents on areas of equal value. If a light tint is placed on a dark surface, it will appear to come forward or make the surface appear to bulge. If a dark accent is placed on a light surface, it will cause the area to recede and may even look like a hole, disrupting all the great value changes you've worked to achieve.

Be sure your tints and accents are softened into the background. You don't want them to jump off the surface, or to look spotty, as if they were an afterthought. When I paint tints and accents I like to imagine the viewer saying, "Is that purple (or green, or yellow) I see?" Tints and accents make the viewer look more closely and linger on the painting, giving them more time to notice all that detail I love to paint. Look at your painting at arm's length—if you see small isolated areas of strong color or can identify spots of color, soften them into the background by adjusting their value, intensity or temperature.

Tints should be placed on areas of equal value. If a tint is too light it makes the surface appear to bulge.

A tint or accent that is too dark for its position on the object will create a depression, and may even cause what appears to be a hole.

Application of Techniques

The following demonstrations show you how to use the painting techniques you've learned in the previous chapters to paint a variety of flower types. Once you know which method works best to create certain characteristic details, you can apply these techniques to any flower. The subject itself, the size of the object, its background values and sometimes the mood I want to convey determines the technique I use.

Zinnia

I decided to use floated color to shade and highlight these zinnias because the petals are small and I would be able to apply the proper value changes easily.

Begin identifying and separating petals with the first shade value. Float the first light value on the petal, flip your brush and repeat the stroke, overlapping this application.

Continue to reinforce dark and light values. Be sure to carry dark values out far enough as you begin to establish stronger cast shadows.

As you continue to raise light values, start to establish the light values that give the illusion the petal is cupping.

Continue to build the darkest darks and lights. Tuck very dark values into triangles where petals overlap. These very dark values make the petals lift off the others. Using the chisel edge of a flat brush or a liner brush, give slight separation to petals. The tips of several petals are highlighted where the light hits them.

Reinforce final darks and lights. Paint the stamen and pistils using bright yellow values. Continue detailing the center, adding a dark center depression and fine line work between petals.

Poinsettia

*M*any times I apply only the first value shading by floating color and continue with other techniques—in this case stippling was used.

The dark value was applied by floating color. Any reinforcement of the dark values would also be floated.

Because the petals are so mottled, it's easy to add the light values using a very damp round brush loaded with a small amount of paint. It's fine if the paint dries unevenly.

Stippling The mottled look of these poinsettia petals was painted using an old scruffy brush loaded in two values of pink, then lightly tapped against the surface to create a stippled effect.

Gaillardia

Painting petals wet in wet isn't the technique I most frequently use, but it works well with such flowers as pinks or gaillardia.

This gaillardia is painted using a wet-in-wet technique. I started by basecoating the whole flower with a light, opaque color because the background was so dark. I applied a heavy coat of the orange-yellow color, dry wiped my brush, then picked up the lighter yellow value in one corner of the brush. Using the chisel edge of the brush, bridge and combine the two values by "skizzling" the brush back and forth.

When dry, shade around the center by floating a darker value. The light tips are reinforced with a more intense yellow.

Dark values are reinforced and petals are separated using the darkest dark. The center is stippled with a small scruffy flat loaded in dark value reds, toned with darker browns. The inner portion of the center is stippled using a dull, dark green.

Fine line work in dark value red is pulled on petals. The outside center ring is lightened using an old scruffy brush to stipple the light value. The stamen and pistils are painted using small irregular yellow-green dabs, and then touched with a darker red dot.

Cattail

*O*f all the painting techniques, I use extender most frequently. It gives me the ability to apply and soften tints and accents, change temperature and gradually build value change—especially on larger areas and in small triangles. I used two different techniques on this cattail: I applied and softened the dark value with a flat brush, and applied the light value with a round brush and then softened it with a larger scruffy brush.

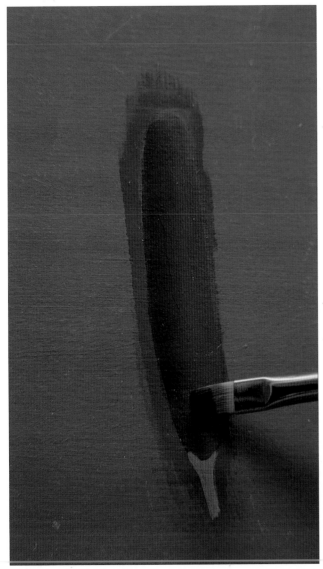

I applied the dark value to the extended area using a flat brush. I then dry wiped the flat brush in the damp area of my paper towel and used it to soften the dark value.

I applied the light value to the extended surface using a small round brush. I then began to soften the light value by patting and pulling over the line using an old scruffy brush that straddles the paint. If a strong line remains, gently slide the scruffy brush sideways, back and forth.

Snapdragon

I used a combination of techniques using extender to paint this snapdragon. When painting a complex flower like the snapdragon, take it apart and paint it section by section.

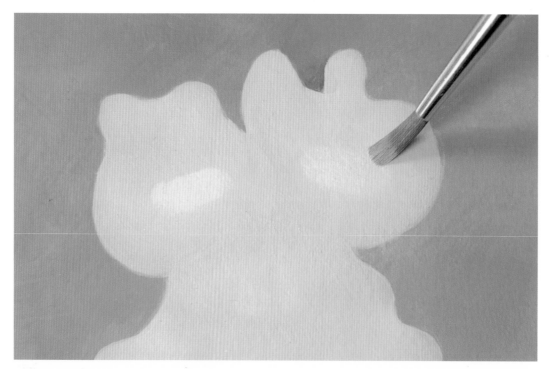

There are many different shapes in the snapdragon. Begin identifying them with soft light and dark values. I applied extender to the surface before setting in light and dark values.

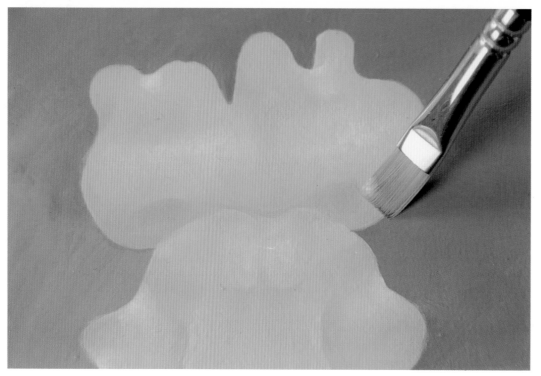

I continued to reinforce light values using a round brush and a soft sable. I began establishing stronger shadow lines with darker values.

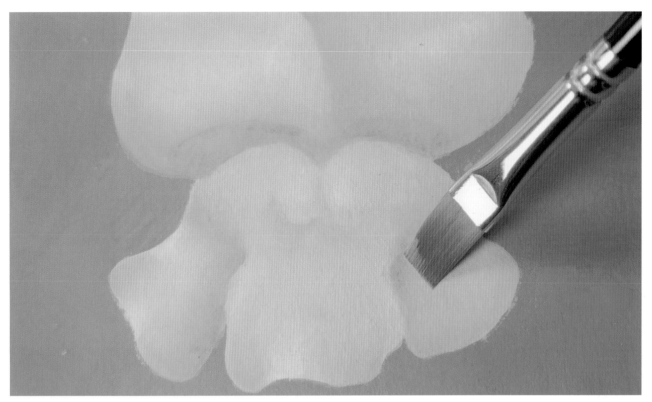

I continued to define and separate petals, developing their individual shapes. Strengthen the shadow area under the top petals.

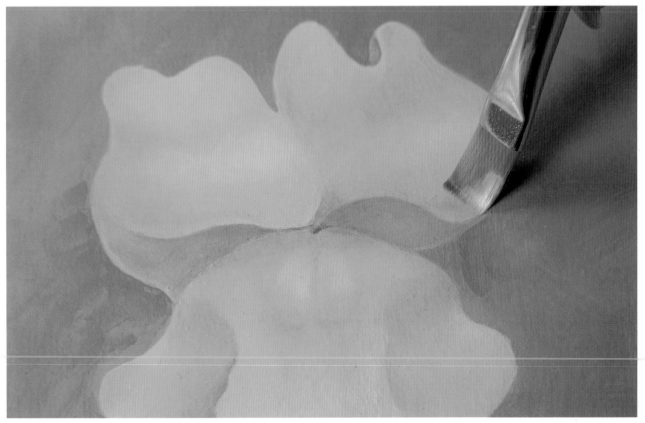

The final details include painting the flower with a light wash of yellow to soften the highlighted areas. I darkened the shadowed areas. I applied stronger yellow tints to the lower petal with Bittersweet. I applied reflected light using black and white.

Sweet Pea

*W*hen petals roll, flip and turn on themselves like the sweet pea, I find it easiest to paint these using a liner brush and extender.

I began to establish the rolls, ruffles and flips with the first dark value. I chose not to apply the first light values at this time because the area is small and, if light and dark values accidently blended together, I would get a muddy or cloudy look. Because the dark value covers less area with the next application, there is less chance of the light and dark values blending. It is safer to apply the first light values in the second step. I applied the dark value to an extended surface using a liner brush to establish the ruffles on the edge and small round brush in the larger rolls.

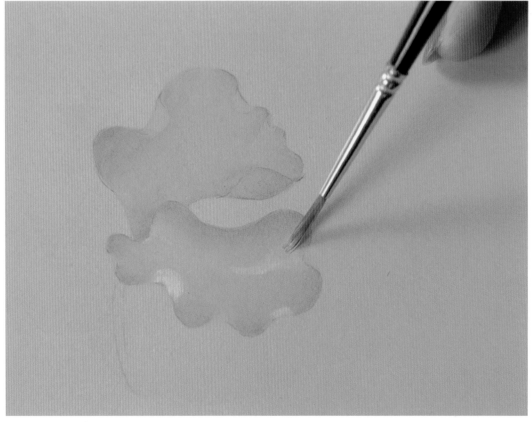

When the paint dried, I began applying the light values and reinforcing the dark values.

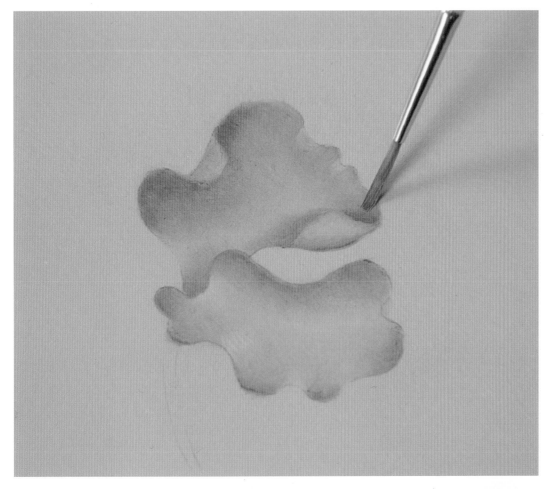

I built the ruffles and rolls along the edge using a liner brush to set the values. I then softened the small triangles using the same brush, once I had dry wiped and flattened it in the damp area of my paper towel. As I built these ruffles and rolls, I worked at keeping them uneven in length and width.

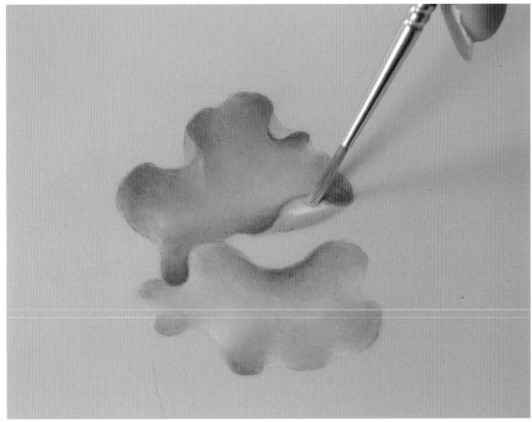

The final details included setting in and softening the small dark areas. I also reinforced the light values on the ruffles, keeping them from becoming too similar. I then painted the reflected light using a smoky blue-gray.

Tulip

Since this tulip is a much larger flower, I was able to paint the highlights using a round brush to apply the paint and a larger sable brush to soften. This required repetition of the same value much of the time. I continued to use extender and a liner brush to establish the small ruffles on the edges. The detailing was painted using a larger round brush and extender. I prefer the round brush over a rake brush because, for me, the rake brush creates a more repetitive look and a liner brush tends to make the details appear more striped.

I started painting this tulip using a warm, medium wash of equal value to the background.

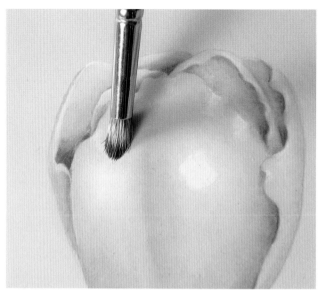

I established the light value area by applying light value to an extended surface with a round brush and softening with a large soft sable. I also began to establish the dark shadow areas inside the petals, along with the light values that establish the ruffles.

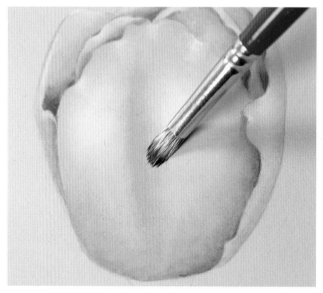

It's necessary to establish a dark value area so the vein will run through. This dark value valley can be set in by painting a darker line on the extended surface and softening with an old scruffy brush or large soft sable.

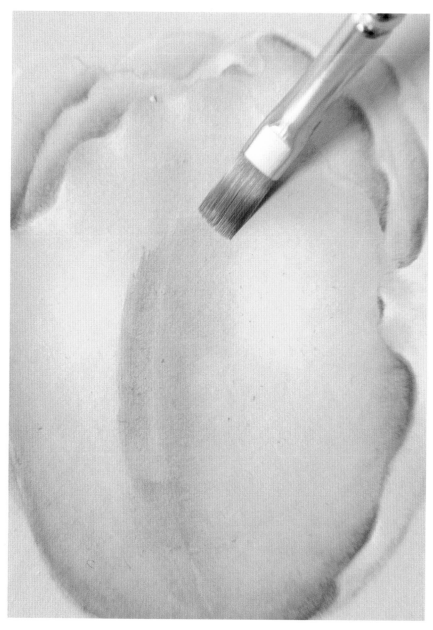

As you continue to soften the dark value, be sure to pull the color out onto the petal in the growth direction. A lighter vein line can be pulled through the dark value. It is necessary to shade and highlight this vein line.

I use a round brush to paint the detail strokes along the edge. Start by loading a round brush in paint. As you dress the brush on your palette, pull and flatten the hairs. This should also leave very little paint in your brush.

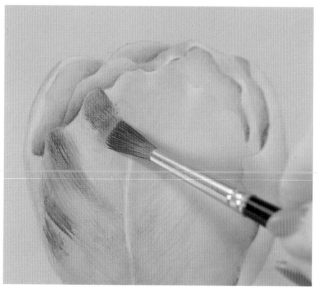

Apply extender to the surface. Starting at the edge, pull strokes onto the body of the flower following the contour of the petals.

Petunia

The petunia is painted with a great deal of detail, using extender to control the value changes. I used the background color to accent the petals on the petunia and help them turn back. Notice the line work flows in the direction the flower grows.

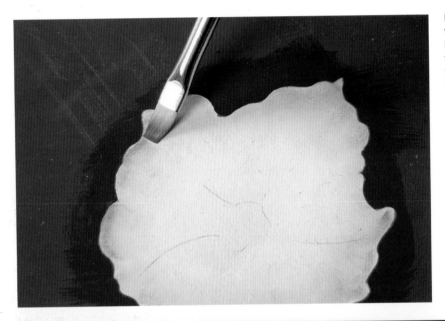

Because I wanted to turn all the petals back from the center, I applied dark value all along the outside edge.

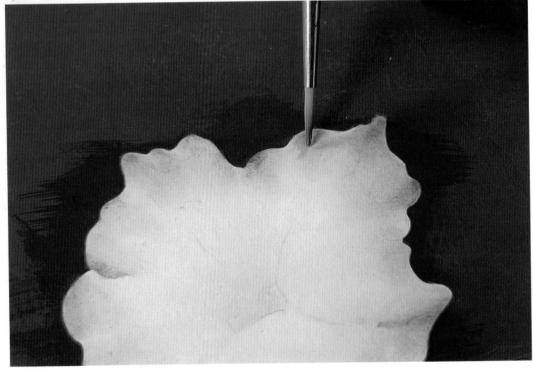

These ruffles are established by identifying where the lightest value will fall and painting darker values on each side.

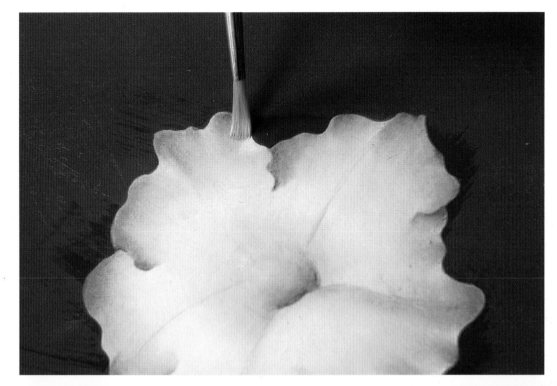

The light values are painted using extender and a round brush, softened with a round sable. The small separations in the petals create a cast shadow. The ruffle will be lighter where it lifts off the petal. I started laying in the center using warm green-yellows. I softly indicated the vein lines in the petals, making sure they flow in the right direction.

I completed the center by darkening into the throat with warm green. More growth lines are pulled using fine yellow-green lines. The stamen and pistils are painted with bright yellow. The background color was used to tint and accent the flower, helping to darken and turn the petals. Warm the flower with a very light wash of yellow, such as Custard.

Balloon Flower

The balloon flower has dark vein lines. In this painting, I have softened the dark lines somewhat so they are not distracting. The center is very fragile and is painted with fine line work.

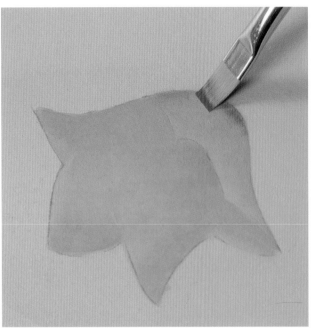

Begin setting up the basic shape of the flower with proper value placement.

This blossom was painted using extender, round and flat brushes. The dark value is placed along the back of the outside edge. The light value is placed in the center area of the two front petals, making them appear to bend forward. Warmer colors were added to the inside shading colors.

The strong vein lines are softly established in the appropriate growth direction. Continue to strengthen dark and light values.

Even though in reality these flowers have dark vein lines, they may be distracting if painted as seen. To soften the lines, I painted over the previously painted line work with a dark value and then softened with a small round sable. I continued to pull fine vein lines in the petals, keeping the value near the value of the petal. The fragile center is painted using fine line work. Keep this value dark enough to prevent it from popping out of the center.

Bachelor's Button

When I'm only floating one color, I don't load the brush with much paint and I use more water. This gives me fainter coverage, one I can use to identify and separate petals. It also provides the opportunity to evaluate and change my mind about the position of specific petals. Generally, when I start out with a light coverage, I expect to repeat or reinforce that application. If you are unhappy with the application of a value because it isn't dark or light enough, repeat that step before moving to the next value.

The petals on this bachelor's button were initially separated by floating color.

I applied extender to the surface to paint the small details and just the light and dark values on this flower. I then touched a liner brush in a small droplet of extender before loading it. I do this to prevent the paint from starting to dry in the liner brush. I dry wiped the liner and used it to soften.

Cool pinks can cause a flower to appear lifeless. The bachelor's button's light value was warmed and enlivened using a scant amount of Custard.

Delphinium

Knowing I wanted a light value background for both the violets and delphinium helped me decide to paint these designs with small amounts of paint and a very damp brush. The very texture of the delphinium, almost a crinkled or crushed tissue paper look, made it easy to paint using this technique.

This delphinium has a light washed basecoat. Begin establishing light and dark values by loading a pinhead of paint in the corner of a very damp flat brush. As you set the brush down, use enough pressure to release the paint and enough water to soften and prevent a drying line.

Build light and dark values using the same technique. Because this technique uses so little paint it may be necessary to repeat steps, but because they dry so quickly the process moves right along.

When a flower appears too cool or lifeless, wash over petals with a very light wash of a yellow, such as Custard. Continue to build dark values.

The flower is complete when the center is detailed with proper value control and the outside tips of the blossom are darkened.

Violets

Because the violets are small, the paint dries rapidly—the first blossoms will be dry by the time the whole design is painted, enabling you to start again with the next value. The intensity of the detail line work is controlled by adding water.

This violet is painted using a light basecoat wash. First value darks are established using a pinhead of paint in the corner of a very damp brush.

The top petals will appear to roll back when a darker value is applied. In this violet, one top petal is more horizontal and the other is more vertical. Placement of the dark values controls this.

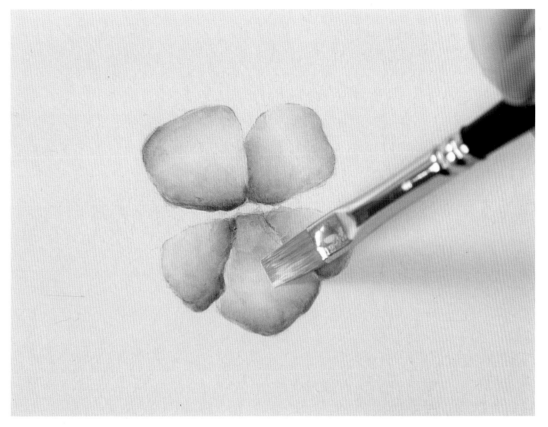

To make the lower petal appear to be growing out from the center and bending, it is necessary to establish a light value across the front of the petal.

The center is painted using a dull green-yellow. The vein lines are painted with very fine lines, mostly visible on the lower petals.

Lily

I used a light yellow wash on this lily to bring the light value areas to life. The growth lines are painted using an old liner brush that has been flattened. The shadows cast by the stamen and pistils reflect the contour of the petal.

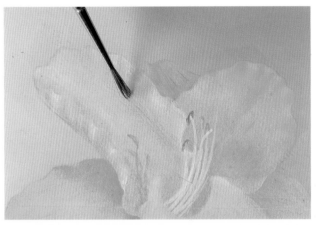

The growth lines are painted with an old liner brush, using duller, darker value. These lines are pulled in the growth direction.

This lily was brightened using a light wash of yellow.

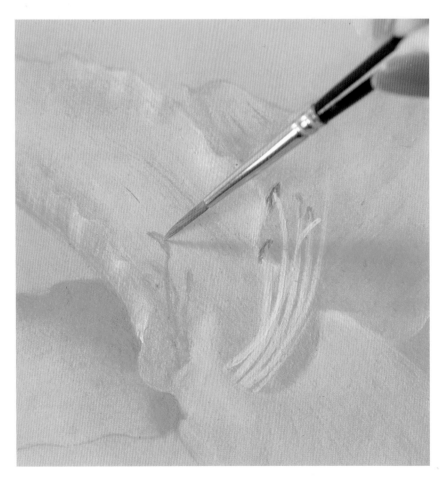

The stamen and pistils cast a shadow on the back petal. These are painted with a duller, darker petal value, and follow the contour of the petal they are on. There are many warm coral color tints. The tiny ruffles are painted with a liner brush using light and dark values and extender.

Rose

The rose has many rolling petals. It presents a challenge when painting warmer, lighter interior petals. It becomes more complicated when painting the cast shadows and creating the illusion of light traveling through the petals. It has strong yellow accents in the interior portion of the lower petals.

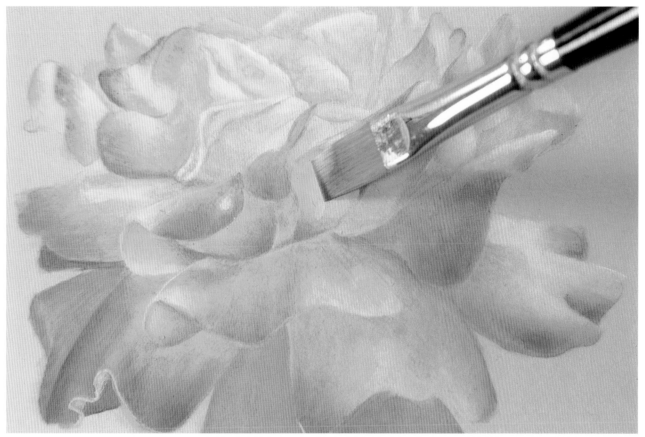

This rose was painted using extender to place and soften tints, accents and shadows. It has lots of tints to create the illusion of light flowing through the petals. There are many yellow accents reflected in the interior section of the lower petals. To avoid too strong an accent, apply the yellow tints softly and gingerly. The cast shadows cause interesting darks and are a challenge because the petals lighten toward the center. Fine line work created the thickness of the petals.

Background and Filler Flowers

Background and filler flowers are the smaller flowers that appear in the background or peripheral areas of a design. Their purpose is to help unify a composition by filling in space, and to connect and support major elements with color, size, direction and even theme. Theirs is a supporting role, and the amount of detail they offer is dictated by their position in a design.

Filler flowers can consist of a small grouping of one type of flower like bachelor's buttons, or a larger, airier type of flower like Queen Anne's lace or baby's breath. Many of the filler-type flowers are individual blossoms in a large cluster, like baby's breath or lilacs. Flowers like baby's breath will have a looser appearance than flowers that are massed together on the stalk like lilacs.

These clusters or masses should be recognized as a basic shape. When painting the individual blossoms, their value is determined by their location in that basic shape. If a smaller cluster comes forward, perhaps in the middle of the mass, it should be painted with lighter values to make it come forward, away from the main body.

If you decide to include flowers like baby's breath in your design, be sure you treat the whole as a basic shape first. When painting small individual flowers, keep them loose and make sure some overlap others—don't make them uniform.

Small stroke work leaves and stems should be added, but it isn't necessary to connect each blossom to a stem. The color green is very important in any of these filler-type flowers. Even if you don't want to paint individual leaves and stems, you still need to create the illusion of having them. By incorporating some green into the background washes, the viewer will automatically see it as foliage.

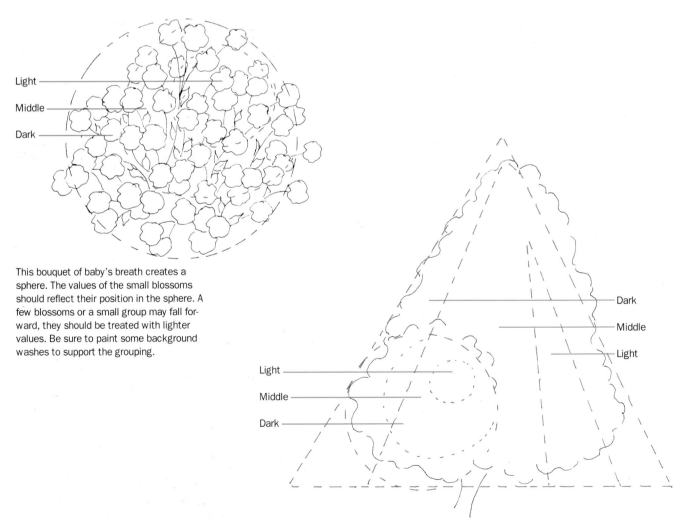

Light
Middle
Dark

This bouquet of baby's breath creates a sphere. The values of the small blossoms should reflect their position in the sphere. A few blossoms or a small group may fall forward, they should be treated with lighter values. Be sure to paint some background washes to support the grouping.

Dark
Middle
Light

Light
Middle
Dark

This lilac forms a triangle; the small area that bulges forward is treated as a sphere.

Loose Filler Flowers

Forget-me-nots, tansy, baby's breath, lilacs, yarrow and Queen Anne's lace are some of the flowers I consider loose filler flowers. The seedpods of some flowers are as pretty and as interesting as the blossoms themselves. The seedpod of love-in-a-mist makes a great filler flower.

If these flowers are located in a peripheral area, I usually begin with very light and loose foliage and flower colors. After this has dried, I may strengthen some of the colors before continuing to softly indicate individual flowers with slightly stronger color. As these flowers come closer to the center of interest, I paint them with more value, intensity and detail. If there are filler flowers located in the center of interest area, I usually paint a few with clean, identifying detail. Many of the loose filler flowers can certainly stand alone in a design. Lilacs, forget-me-nots and yarrow are only a few of the filler flowers that can be painted individually and in close range.

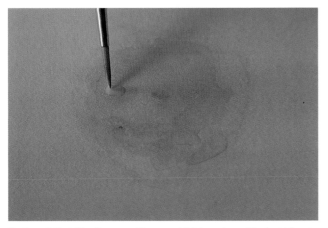

Begin painting filler flowers with several light washes of leaf and flower colors. Let them bleed together. Control the outside drying lines by touching edges with a clean, wet brush. Reinforce the washes, setting up areas where flower petals may fall.

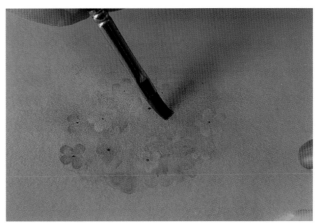

Begin setting in small petals. Keep them loose and few in number. Let the viewer assume the washes are the flowers and foliage. Sometimes just setting down a faint center in loose color will give the illusion of a flower.

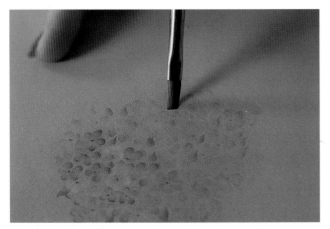

The middle plane will have more flowers. These flowers will have more value changes and be more intense, but will not carry lots of detail.

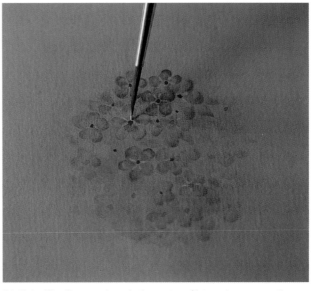

Of all the filler flowers, those in the center of interest area carry the most detail. Remember, filler flowers are only supporting members, not the main event.

Fluff Flowers

I refer to flowers having a massed appearance like lavender, spiraea, artemisia, statice or bridal wreath as fluff flowers. I see them as a basic shape but, because the blossoms are so small, it is next to impossible to paint any individual blossoms. Be careful to paint these basic shapes well and, if possible, paint any identifying characteristics. For example, indicate the natural curve of German statice, a few dark centers on the bridal wreath or tiny round seedpods on the artemisia. The viewer will recognize the flower by the color, shape and unique characteristics.

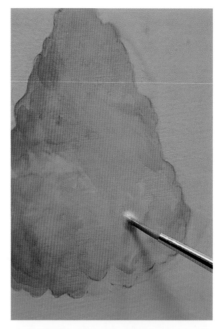

If you're painting a large form, it may be necessary to first basecoat with a wash of medium value. Continue by applying shading and light value. When that is dry, begin to add foliage and flower color in small dabs using a heavy wash consistency. Let dry.

Look for areas in the background that lend themselves to forming petals. Paint the petals with a flat brush, corner loaded in a scant amount of paint of the appropriate value. Each petal is created by painting a small "C" stroke, reinforcing as necessary. All four petals will not be visible in each flower. Set petals in loosely, starting at outside edges and working toward the lightest value area, where most of the full four-petaled flowers will be located.

Filler flowers in the center of interest will be more refined and carry more detail. Finish the detail by adding line work to any buds, dividing them into four sections. Add shading to petals, and line work to any petal edge that curls onto itself. Centers are small dabs of yellow toned with any of the purple colors on the palette.

Color, stalk and the arrangement of flowers on the stalk identify this lavender. Pull a few stems in a gray-green color to give it direction. Blossoms are painted using a wet brush, loaded in a pinhead of dark blue. Use pressure to release the paint and water in a small crescent shape.

Reinforce blossoms using lighter value lavender. Set in more blossoms where necessary to fill out the grouping. Stems and blossoms are connected using a flat brush, loaded half in dark blue and half in gray-green. Using the chisel edge, "skizzle" back and forth between stems and blossoms.

Filler flowers can also be painted individually. It may be necessary to enlarge the flowers so all the detail can be appreciated.

Leaves

Just like filler flowers, leaves, stems and tendrils are secondary to the main flowers. They should never be as important as the flowers they support. Leaves grow in all different shapes and sizes and may vary on the same flower stem.

When I paint leaves I always want them to relate to the flower they belong to, which may mean studying and taking notes on certain leaves. I've found it a great help to photocopy leaves, and sometimes even flowers, to use as a reference when I'm unsure of the exact shape or of their edges and veins.

Leaves have many different shapes, and these shapes should be used to their best advantage. The leaves on cosmos and Queen Anne's lace are loose and airy. They may work best in peripheral areas, while larger, heavier leaves work best when used to support heavier flowers.

Lupine and geranium leaves are identifying characteristics of their flowers. In cases like these it would be a good idea to include at least part of the leaf, painted accurately, in your design.

Like filler flowers, leaves can help connect and balance a design with color, shape and direction. Don't limit your selection of leaves to those that belong to flowers; consider the foliage from vines, like ivy or vinca vine, or fern-type leaves.

Small violet leaf

Lilac leaf

Large violet leaf

Cosmos leaf

Pansy leaf

Black-eyed Susan leaf

Veins

Veins on leaves are as different as the leaves themselves. Some veins are barely visible, such as on a tulip leaf. Others may have one central vein with small veins branching off, like a rose leaf. The small branches may be directly opposite each other or they may branch off the center vein in regularly staggered or in irregular intervals.

The size of the leaf and its location in the composition determines how visible these small branches are when painted. If you do decide to paint side veins don't be timid or they will appear as an after thought.

Some leaves have several large veins starting at the stem end instead of one main vein. The zinnia leaf is one example. The small veins on a violet leaf branch off larger veins, but only on the side toward the outside edge. The main vein may be large, bulging and so obvious it will require value change. This bulge is usually obvious on the underside of a leaf. In the majority of the leaves I paint, the main vein exists in a depression, which is generally referred to in decorative painting as a "gully." This gully runs through the center of the leaf. Because it is a depression, it will carry darker values. When combined with the darker values at the bottom of a leaf, the gully sets up what is often referred to in decorative painting as an "anchor."

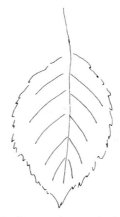

The rose leaf has a main central vein with side veins branching off at regular and equal intervals.

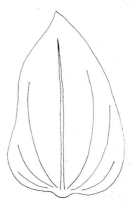

Some leaves, like this zinnia leaf, have several large veins originating at the stem end.

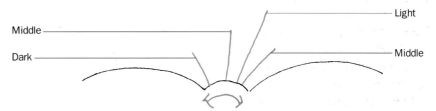

Seen mostly on the underside of leaves, these large veins need value change when located in the center of interest area.

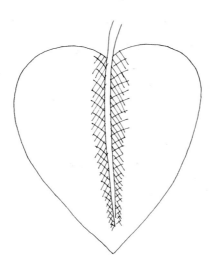

A center vein is usually located in a small, dark value depression, or gully, running through the center of the leaf.

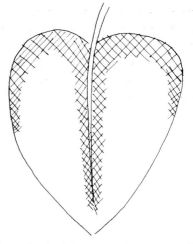

Combining the dark values at the stem end of the leaf, the dark values in the center vein area and the dark value on the upper side edges creates the "anchor" shape.

$\mathcal{N}$o matter how the veins grow in a specific leaf, they should all be painted with a graceful flow in the appropriate direction. Like limbs on a tree, which usually grow toward the sun on one main trunk, pull side veins out from the main vein and toward the tip of the leaf. When you're pulling a vein, keep in mind that the vein has to line up with the leaf's stem.

Stroke Work Leaves

Smaller leaves, like cosmos and bachelor's button leaves, or leaves closer to a blossom may be too small to paint with value change or great detail. It is best to paint them with graceful strokes of line work that have good temperature and intensity control. Any value change would be limited to a quick application, almost a dry brush, of a light value. The calyx may be treated similarly if it is not in the center of interest, or is in a position with little exposure.

There are generic leaves that work well in any area of the design, and they can include as much detail as the location dictates. There are also some very effective generic stroke work leaves. The configuration, number and size communicate to the viewer what they are. Add a vein or some other little detail and you're done. Stroke work leaves appear more natural and flowing if you don't trace on every leaf—maybe just the main stem.

It isn't necessary to paint tremendous value changes on small leaves and stems. A quick, light value will be enough.

These stroke work leaves are good for filling in peripheral areas. Start with the chisel edge of your brush in a horizontal line and apply pressure.

Rotate the brush until it is vertical.

Let the hairs come together and lift straight off.

Pull a vein line and you're finished.

Leaf Details

While studying leaves, I noticed that many have jagged or sawtooth edges. The larger the leaf, the more pronounced the jagged edge, as seen with violet leaves. The classic jagged-edge leaf is on a rose. In addition to being jagged, the edge is almost always accented, another identifying characteristic that should be painted. At times I have used the darker edge color to help clean up and clarify the saw-tooth appearance.

Paint jagged edges using the chisel edge of your brush and "skizzling" back and forth.

Strengthen the edges with a darker value.

Finally, clean and crisp up edges with strong color.

The main vein has to line up with the stem.

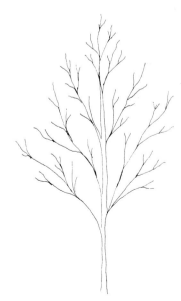

When in doubt as to which way to pull side veins, think of a tree. Just as the limbs grow to the top, pull the secondary veins to the tip of the leaf. Don't be tempted to pull a vein out and back because the leaf seems to roll that way. Keep the tip of the leaf pointing toward you and pull the veins toward you.

To add variety in the center of interest area, I will roll, flip or curl a leaf. When I do this I always want it to be believable, not overdone. Some leaves curl and flip whether they are located in the center of interest area or not. The most obvious is a tulip leaf. The length of lily and iris leaves causes them to bend, invariably exposing the underside of the leaf. This is generally of a lighter value and at some point the thickness of the edge will be visible. No matter how the leaf rolls, flips or curls, each has to be treated as a basic shape and painted accordingly.

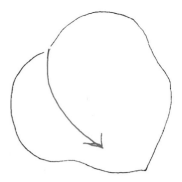

This leaf will appear to roll onto its side because of the center vein placement. Vary the vein placement to make a group of leaves interesting. Because of the larger surface area there is opportunity to include a bug bite, a water droplet or more detailed veining.

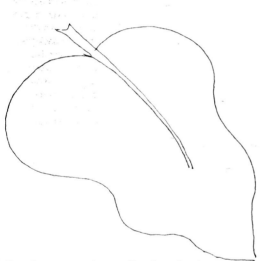

The edges on many leaves will curl or roll and dip. This gives the opportunity to make a leaf more interesting through value change.

Large leaves often flip or turn onto themselves. If you decide to flip a leaf and are painting veins, be sure the vein on the underside appears to line up with the vein on top.

Thickness of edge.

As a leaf bends or flips, at some point the thickness of the edge will be apparent.

As this lily leaf bends the edge becomes apparent and is painted with a lighter value. The exposed underside is also painted with a lighter value. What appears to be a vein is painted with a darker value.

In addition to rolls and flips, a bug bite is another natural leaf detail. I would caution against large, multiple bug bites, especially when you want your viewer to see beautiful, healthy flowers. Before you paint bug bites, take a minute to think about the damage a bug bite would cause. The edges of the leaf would die where it was bitten, causing them to turn brown and lifeless. Rather than painting a lifeless, irregular circle around the bug bite, which could look dull, vary it with a complementary color.

Also ask yourself what color the area showing through the bug bite would be. If it's on top of another leaf, it would be dark green. But what if it's located in an area that has light behind it? If the latter is the case, remember that because the bug bite is so small, whatever light is visible will be darker and duller.

Placing values on leaves can become confusing when a leaf is tucked under a flower or rolls side to side and stem end to tip. Remember to locate your basic shapes, then add three value changes to create form. Once you've done that, consider the value change caused by a cast shadow. If you have a leaf that rolls in two directions, lay out the value placement and it will become obvious the lightest area on the leaf is where the two light value areas combine. If you don't want a leaf to appear flat or head straight into the background, you have to place darker value on the tip to turn it down.

Before you divide your leaf into sections for value placement, consider the position, size and direction of its neighbors. Don't paint them all the same—have one rolling more, one more on its side or one with the center vein hidden. You can control this by planning where your vein line will fall. In a grouping of leaves, be sure to vary the direction you pull the main veins. You will get a pinwheel effect if every vein is headed in the same direction.

I generally include warm, cool and neutral leaves in more involved designs. Comparing the temperature of a leaf to the temperature of the color scheme, and comparing each leaf's temperature to the others, determines how warm or cool a leaf appears. If the colors of the leaves seem too dull or lifeless, remember most living things are yellow-green.

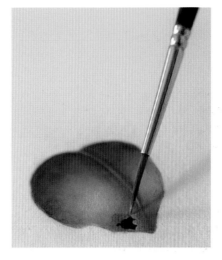

The hole created by a bug bite on a dark surface is painted a dark value. Paint it in an irregular shape to make it more interesting. The edge around the bite is painted a light brown to indicate where the leaf is dying.

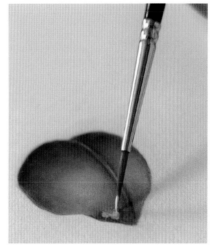

The area behind this leaf is just atmosphere—indicate this with a value slightly darker and duller than the background color. The dried, dead area around this bite is made stronger with the application of a darker, dull red.

Plan various vein placements. This makes each leaf different and helps prevent you from dividing leaves in half. Variety adds interest.

If you paint each vein in the same direction you will paint what looks like a pinwheel.

On small filler leaves, I may choose to paint the tip with cool colors to help it recede, with background color to help it settle into the background, or warmer colors to keep it forward. If the value of this color remains lighter on the tip, the leaf will appear to go straight off, not bending, and sometimes this is what I want. If I am painting on a light value background, I like to basecoat leaves using a light wash. This allows me to build the dark values and use the background value as the first value light.

Separate these leaves by making some warmer with a color equal in value to the background. Create lost edges by washing the background color over the tip. Put one behind the other with a wash of cool color equal in value to the background.

When painting washed leaves on a light background, I start with one or two light washes.

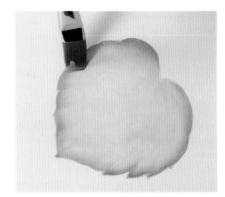

I continue by establishing a darker value along the outside edge. This darker value is often the base color of the wash; because it is not a wash consistency it appears darker.

As I build the outside edges with darker values it becomes necessary to apply more washes to the leaf to prevent a striped look. Apply these washes gradually, only covering the areas you want darker, leaving the background value as the light value.

Clean up the outside edge with a dark value and reinforce the light value with light washes. Float one side of the vein using a small flat brush loaded with a pinhead of paint. Repeat along the other side, creating a narrow light value vein, which is in reality the background. If any veins appear too dark, apply a light wash of the background value.

I use stroke work to paint a group of small rose leaves. Cosmos leaves, bachelor's button leaves and some calyxes can also be painted using strokes.

Generally, I basecoat large supporting leaves opaquely. Shading and highlighting can be painted using extender. Details can be painted using a liner brush and extender.

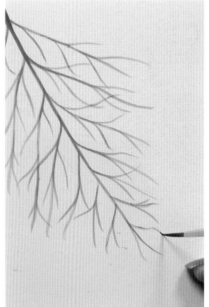

I would paint this small group of rose leaves using a basic stroke and an indication of a vein. The number and configuration help identify these as rose leaves.

On a light value background rose leaves can be stroked using a small flat brush that is corner loaded. "Skizzle" back and forth while rotating the brush from a horizontal position to a vertical position. Add stem and vein lines.

Cosmos leaves are painted using a liner brush, keeping them graceful and airy. They work great as a filler leaf, loosening up a design.

This calyx can be stroked on. If it is in the center of interest area, more dark and light values could be added.

Zinnia Leaf

Rose Leaf

When painting large supporting leaves near the center of interest, I begin by basecoating them opaquely. I then apply the first dark value using floated color or by extending the area and then dark value. This first application is on the stem end and tip of a multiveined leaf like the zinnia. The "anchor" shape is apparent on the rose leaf.

Continue building dark values and establish the first value light. I find it helpful to indicate the vein lines at this time.

Zinnia Leaf

Rose Leaf

The next step includes reinforcing the dark values if necessary and applying the second value light. Begin building dark value along vein lines where necessary.

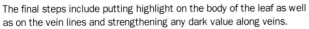

The final steps include putting highlight on the body of the leaf as well as on the vein lines and strengthening any dark value along veins.

Stems

When you look at stems it's amazing how interesting they are. Many stems have teeny-tiny hairs on them. Some are loaded with prickly thorns.

If you're painting rose stems, you'll have to plan on painting the thorns. Study how they grow off the stem and where and how the temperature and values change. Again, this would be a minor detail.

On the occasions when stems are visible, they should be painted as cylinders, with appropriate value change. Branches and stems in some instances are what I call woody. When I paint these, I like to use dark brown and warm green loaded (but not dressed) in a liner brush. This allows both colors to be present in the branch or stem. Besides warm green, red-browns and cool grays may be present in stems. Study a rose stem to see these color variations.

This photo shows the thorns on a rose stem with just a hint of light value on the tip of the thorns and where they connect to the stem.

In areas where value change is not of major importance, try painting branches or woody stems with a liner brush loaded in brown and warm green. Dress the brush to remove any excess paint, keeping both colors as clean as possible. When you pull the line the two colors combine to give enough brown for a wood feel and yet enough green to keep it alive.

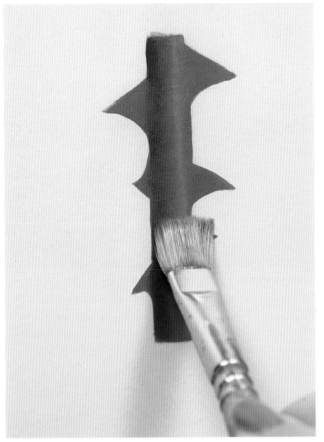

Branches should be treated as cylinders with three value changes.

The placement of the thorns should be random. A hint of a tip will give the impression that they grow all around the branch. These can be basecoated, but I would stroke smaller thorns with a dull red.

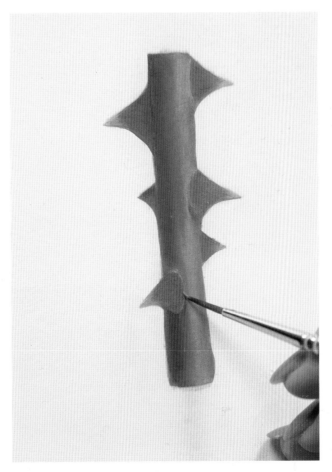

Add the light values on the tips and around where the thorn is connected to the branch.

Tendrils

Many of my students moan when they have to paint tendrils, especially since I don't let them trace the tendrils from a pattern. I encourage my students not to trace the tendrils because it is very hard to follow the tracing and make the tendrils appear graceful. If you feel you have to have some guidelines, I suggest making a few dots along the way—maybe at the beginning, middle and end of the line work—then connecting them freehand. This will help you achieve a more natural look.

When you paint the tendrils, remember that they are lines and will direct a viewer's eye. Be sure your tendrils end facing toward your center of interest, not off the edge or curling straight up.

Tendrils should vary in thickness and have proper value change. When painting value change on narrow line work, apply it after the line work dries. Determine where the line work bulges forward and where it turns under. Extender, wet brush and dry brush techniques can all be used to apply these values. Whichever method you choose, be sure the light value is applied to the bulging area and dark values are applied where the tendril turns away from the light source.

I'm convinced if you load an appropriately sized liner brush correctly, you will paint great line work. Don't forget you must have water to transport paint out of a liner brush. In order for a brush to hold water, you have to have enough hairs or bristles to hold the paint and water. Have you ever tried painting tiny line work and instead ended up with stuttered, thick globs? You were probably using the wrong brush or didn't take the time to load it with the right consistency of paint. You must also hold the brush so the paint and water flow off the tip of the brush—make sure you keep the brush perpendicular to the surface, supporting it with your pinkie.

Light and dark values are obvious on these sweet pea tendrils.

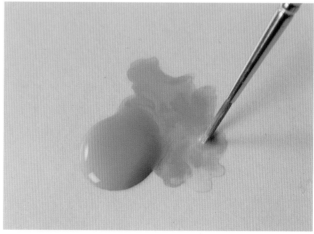

When you load a liner brush, pull the paint out and add enough droplets of water to make it the consistency of heavy cream. Before leaving your palette, test to see if you have the right consistency of paint in your brush. If you can't pull a thin, fine line, you need more water. Don't rinse the brush, just pick up a droplet of water from your palette.

To paint great tendrils the paint has to flow off the tip of the brush. Hold your brush perpendicular to the surface, supporting it with your pinky finger.

Common Line Work Problems

- When painting tendrils, the line work has a tendency to crimp just when you're going around a corner. This happens when you don't slow down for the curves.
- You might get a little flick just when you're ending the best tendril you've ever painted. To keep this from happening, stop as you end your tendril to let the hairs of the brush come together and lift straight off.
- Lots of times the brush is loaded just fine but the line work appears thick and watery. Rather than rinsing and reloading your brush, blot it at the ferrule on the fold of a paper towel.

If you don't slow down while you are creating a loop in your line work you're liable to paint a crimp in it. Go slowly when you're painting loops and they'll be more graceful. If you are too timid with the line work it will appear weak. Add light and dark values as the tendril rolls.

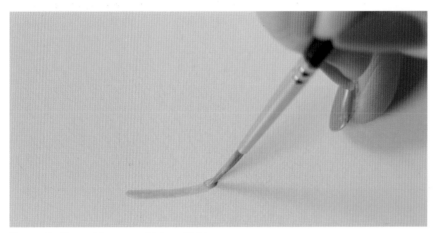

If you pull a line and it appears thick and light, you are carrying too much water in your brush.

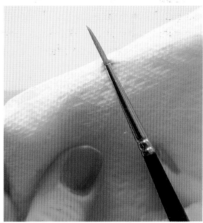

Don't rinse, just pick up your paper towel and blot the brush at the ferrule.

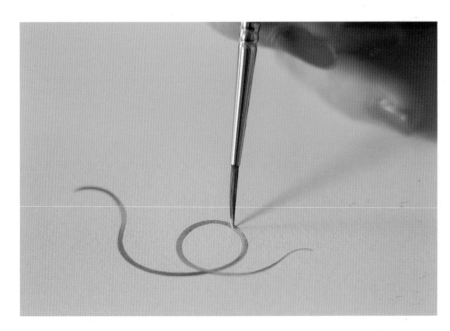

Use any one of several techniques to add lights and shadows to a tendril.

Flower Colors

I have explained how I approach different petals, centers and shaped flowers. You can apply any or all of that information to any flower you want. Whether it has a cupped petal, a flipped petal or it's a sphere or cone, you can use the rules I have given you to understand how to paint it, where to place the different values and how to add interest with washes and temperature change.

As you start out, you may wish to try some of the following color options I have found successful. These colors may appear intense here but when thinned with water or extender, they will relate well. As you gain confidence, don't be afraid to experiment on your own and trust your instincts. Remember, you dress yourself and your young children, you decorate your house and you do a good job! If you feel a color is too yellow or too cool, change it using the information I have given you.

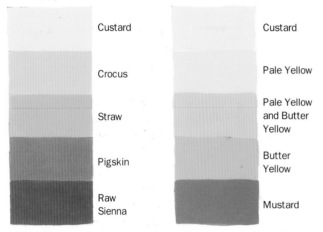

Yellow Flowers Consider using these colors when painting yellow flowers. To paint lighter, more lemon colored flowers I use cooler yellows with shading values leaning toward yellow-green.

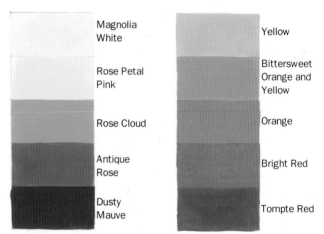

Red Flowers The following are choices for color when painting red flowers. Whether you paint cool or warm red flowers, remember the dark and light values can be reinforced with lighter or darker values.

Blue Flowers The following are color choices used for painting blue flowers. Many of the flowers we consider blue actually lean toward violet or red-violet. The color can be adjusted by adding tints and accents.

White Flowers The following are color suggestions for painting white flowers. Because living things are generally yellow-green, I use yellow-green for shading. When it's necessary to paint cooler whites, I use gray-blues to shade. Although not shown here, I like to use a warm, light Custard in one of the light values to bring the flower to life.

Putting it All Together

When you are designing a composition remember there are certain flowers that work better together than others. For instance, if your main flowers are daisies, your best choice for secondary flowers would not be chrysanthemums—they are too similar. A better choice would be flowers with petals of a different shape, size and number. You might want to use filler type flowers to add height and give the composition an airier feeling.

When planning a composition, my first consideration is line. I want a composition that flows gracefully and creates movement. I generally choose an "S" or "C" curve. Once I establish the line, I quickly draw in the main mass area and perhaps a few smaller areas. After I have established these mass areas, I look to see what space is around them and ask, "Is it airy enough, should I pull it apart more, do I see any straight or even lines?" I don't want the space to be too even or linear or too cluttered.

I then start to plan what flowers work in the mass areas. I think about color, size, value and the amount of detail each has. How much of the center will show? Is it interesting? Does it have strong vein lines? I may exclude a flower because it just wouldn't lay naturally in a certain position or direction.

While I am deciding which flowers to use, I always think of the center of interest area and try to pick flowers and leaves that will enable me to paint the darkest darks and lightest lights. I choose a flower with a color that works throughout the painting in varying intensity and temperature. I call that color the "mother" color because it is the main or dominant color of the painting and everything else is in relationship to that color.

A flower can dominate a painting with its size, value, intensity, number and detail. I choose a flower I can paint all that detail on, with less and less detail as I move away from the center of interest. I also want the remaining flowers to work well with the main flower in size, shape and number of petals to create harmony, balance and interest.

The information I have included in this book was meant to show you how I paint realistic details on flowers and how I use details to draw and keep the viewer's attention. Is there ever a point when there is too much detail? The answer is yes. If you overdo the details your painting can become stiff, boring or hard—and when you love the details it is easy to do.

Remember to keep the most detail in the center of interest and as you move away use less and less. The outer areas can still look real without being distracting.

When I first started learning these rules, I remember thinking I'd never see a triangle in a ruffle or circle in a rose. If you find yourself getting caught up in the rules or becoming uptight, just relax. Use your imagination and trust your own creative instincts. Remember that rules are made to be broken and just paint a pretty picture!

Index